touchPOINTS™ *for Those Who Serve*

touchPOINTS™

— for —

THOSE WHO SERVE

TYNDALE HOUSE PUBLISHERS, INC.
CAROL STREAM, ILLINOIS

PEACE PRAYER

O Lord, even when we are at war, make us instruments
  of your peace.
Where there is hatred, let us plant the seeds of your love;
  Where there is injury, . . . pardon;
  Where there is doubt, . . . faith;
  Where there is despair, . . . hope;
  Where there is darkness, . . . light;
  Where there is sadness, . . . joy.

O Lord, even when we are at war, make us instruments
  of your peace.
Where there is injustice, let us plant the seeds of justice;
  Where there is pride, . . . humility;
  Where there is anger, . . . restraint;
  Where there is brutality, . . . kindness;
  Where there is fear, . . . courage;
  Where there is blindness, . . . wisdom.

O Lord, even when we are at war, make us instruments
  of your peace.
Take the good seeds that we plant,
  And grow them into good blessings
  For the sake of your Name and your Kingdom.

Amen.

(INSPIRED BY THE PEACE PRAYER ATTRIBUTED TO FRANCIS OF ASSISI)

Visit Tyndale online at www.tyndale.com.

TYNDALE, Tyndale's quill logo, *New Living Translation*, *NLT*, and the New Living Translation logo are registered trademarks of Tyndale House Publishers, Inc.

TouchPoints is a trademark of Tyndale House Publishers, Inc.

TouchPoints for Those Who Serve

Questions and notes copyright © 2012 by Ronald A. Beers. All rights reserved.

Some material has been taken from previous *TouchPoints* editions.

General editor: Bonne Steffen

Contributing writers: V. Gilbert Beers, Rebecca Beers, Ronald A. Beers, Brian R. Coffey, Jonathan Farrar, Jonathan Gray, Sean A. Harrison, Sandy Hull, Amy E. Mason, Rhonda K. O'Brien, Douglas J. Rumford, Bonne Steffen, Linda Taylor

Designed by Jennifer Ghionzoli

Cover photograph of flag copyright © Beathen/Corbis. All rights reserved

Cover eagle artwork © Fortunepig78/Shutterstock. All rights reserved.

Scripture quotations are taken from the *Holy Bible*, New Living Translation, copyright © 1996, 2004, 2007 by Tyndale House Foundation. Used by permission of Tyndale House Publishers, Inc., Carol Stream, Illinois 60188. All rights reserved.

ISBN 978-1-4143-7108-5

Printed in the United States of America

18	17	16	15	14	13	12
7	6	5	4	3	2	1

CONTENTS

FOREWORD

Those of us who have worn the "cloth of our country" and served in the military know it is a unique experience. We belong to a group of amazing men and women who epitomize the word *service*—making sacrifices for purposes beyond promoting self-interest. While these experiences can be rewarding, they also can be intensely demanding—physically, mentally, and spiritually. Lengthy deployments add to the challenges.

Whether your rank is senior or junior, whether you serve as a chaplain or are a family member on the home front, there will always be uncertainties involved in this unique lifestyle. And where there are uncertainties, there are questions. The Bible provides answers to these questions, but how do you know where to look? *TouchPoints for Those Who Serve* helps fill this need. With topics arranged alphabetically from "Abilities" to "Worth," it's easy to get right to the pressing issue. Additionally, each topic ends with a "Promise from God," a welcome encouragement because God never breaks his promises.

Military men and women never seem to have much time, so this is an ideal resource for finding quick answers on tough issues. Proverbs 3:6 says, "Seek his will in all you do, and he will show you which path to take." My prayer is that this small book may help you draw closer to God and show you how deeply he cares for you, no matter what your circumstances.

Rear Admiral Curtis Kemp, US Navy (Ret)
Board Chairman, Cadence International

WITH THANKS TO
ALL SERVICE MEMBERS

It is our privilege to publish *Touchpoints for Those Who Serve* in gratitude for you, the men and women who defend our country's freedom both here and abroad. Not only are the people of this nation indebted to all members of the armed services for selfless sacrifice, the world is also in your debt. The training you have undergone has prepared you for the situations you have been called to face, especially those that put you in harm's way. Please know that many people—family, friends, and those you've never met—continually hold you in their hearts and uphold you in their prayers.

If you find yourself struggling at any time, we hope that you will look for answers in this book and will talk with a trusted confidant or a chaplain. Most important, "Seek the LORD while you can find him. Call on him now while he is near" (Isaiah 55:6).

The Editors

INTRODUCTION

PSALM 119:105 | *Your word is a lamp to guide my feet and a light for my path.*

The topics you'll find in *TouchPoints for Those Who Serve* have been specifically selected to address and give biblical advice on some of the most pressing issues that affect service members today. Each section begins with introductory questions. Answers are drawn from the Bible, followed by concise commentary that further explains the biblical insight, and ending with a "Promise from God." These elements combine to show how relevant the Bible is to today's concerns, giving solid guidance for daily living whether you are at home or far from loved ones. The topics are presented in alphabetical order, with a complete listing of the topics in the table of contents for quick reference. In many cases, topics are cross-referenced to related topics.

Whether you read through this book page by page or use it as a reference for topics of particular interest to you, may you find answers in God's Word as you make it your daily guide.

ABILITIES

Where do my abilities come from?

EXODUS 31:1-3 | *The LORD said to Moses, "Look, I have specifically chosen Bezalel. . . . I have filled him with the Spirit of God, giving him great wisdom, ability, and expertise in all kinds of crafts."*

DEUTERONOMY 8:18 | *Remember the LORD your God. He is the one who gives you power to be successful, in order to fulfill the covenant he confirmed to your ancestors with an oath.*

JOHN 15:5 | *[Jesus said,] "Apart from me you can do nothing."*

1 CORINTHIANS 4:7 | *What gives you the right to make such a judgment? What do you have that God hasn't given you? And if everything you have is from God, why boast as though it were not a gift?*

There are no self-made people. God gives each one of us the ability to accomplish our duties and to provide for our needs. You are a steward of those talents.

What does God expect me to do with my abilities?

MATTHEW 25:29 | *To those who use well what they are given, even more will be given, and they will have an abundance. But from those who do nothing, even what little they have will be taken away.*

God has entrusted resources to you according to your ability. He expects you to maximize the effectiveness of those abilities in proportion to his gifting. While the most talented people may seem the most blessed, they must also bear the most responsibility.

JOHN 17:4 | *[Jesus said,] "I brought glory to you here on earth by completing the work you gave me to do."*

Jesus' mission in life was pleasing the Father. This is the ultimate purpose of every person—to bring glory to God through all you say and do, in all times, places, and circumstances.

How can my abilities and even my successes be a danger?

DEUTERONOMY 8:11-14 | *Beware that in your plenty you do not forget the LORD your God and disobey his commands, regulations, and decrees that I am giving you today. For when you have become full and prosperous and have built fine homes to live in, and when your flocks and herds have become very large and your silver and gold have multiplied along with everything else, be careful! Do not become proud at that time and forget the LORD your God.*

When your ability brings you good success and blessing, you are in danger of falling into complacency, forgetting that God gave you your abilities and that you are to consistently use them to serve him and others. Another danger of having great ability is to think you no longer need help or advice from others.

1 CORINTHIANS 1:26-29 | *Remember, dear brothers and sisters, that few of you were wise in the world's eyes or powerful or wealthy when God called you. Instead, God chose things the world considers foolish in order to shame those who think they are wise. And he chose things that are powerless to shame those who are powerful. God chose things despised by the world, things counted as nothing at all, and used them to bring to nothing what the world considers important. As a result, no one can ever boast in the presence of God.*

Your abilities can be liabilities. Within each ability lie the seeds of problems that will sprout if you neglect that ability, use it for your own selfish designs, or presume to rely on it apart from God.

Do my limited abilities limit my ability to serve?

2 CHRONICLES 20:12 | *O our God, won't you stop them? We are powerless against this mighty army that is about to attack us. We do not know what to do, but we are looking to you for help.*

Jehoshaphat, king of Judah, was overwhelmed by the attack coming against the nation because he knew his abilities and resources were no match for those of the enemies. But God opened the way to success. Leaders understand that availability and dependence on the Lord are as important as ability.

PSALM 147:10-11 | *He takes no pleasure in the strength of a horse or in human might. No, the LORD's delight is in those who fear him, those who put their hope in his unfailing love.*

God is not impressed by your abilities or your resources, but by your faith in him.

ZECHARIAH 4:6 | *It is not by force nor by strength, but by my Spirit, says the LORD of Heaven's Armies.*

When facing the most threatening obstacles, the Lord assures you that his ability, not your own, is the ultimate assurance of success.

Promise from God LUKE 12:48 | *When someone has been given much, much will be required in return; and when someone has been entrusted with much, even more will be required.*

ACCOMPLISHMENTS

See also **AMBITION, GOALS**

How can I do a better job of accomplishing things?

ISAIAH 25:1 | *LORD, I will honor and praise your name, for you are my God. You do such wonderful things! You planned them long ago, and now you have accomplished them.*

Accomplishments come with good planning. God planned before he accomplished, providing a good model for you to follow.

ECCLESIASTES 4:9 | *Two people are better off than one, for they can help each other succeed.*

Accomplishments can be multiplied through teamwork. Two people can do even more than twice as much as one, as long as they are pulling in the same direction.

Is it wrong to be proud of my accomplishments?

2 THESSALONIANS 1:11 | *May [God] give you the power to accomplish all the good things your faith prompts you to do.*

Accomplishments bring a sense of personal satisfaction, which is healthy. Always be aware of God's part in enabling you to reach your goals and thank him for what he has done through you. It is arrogant to think you accomplished something all by yourself.

Promise from God PSALM 60:12 | *With God's help we will do mighty things.*

ACCOUNTABILITY

See also **SELF-CONTROL**

How do I become more accountable?

PSALM 1:1 | *Oh, the joys of those who do not follow the advice of the wicked.*

PROVERBS 5:13 | *Oh, why didn't I listen to my teachers? Why didn't I pay attention to my instructors?*

PROVERBS 12:15 | *Fools think their own way is right, but the wise listen to others.*

PROVERBS 27:6 | *Wounds from a sincere friend are better than many kisses from an enemy.*

Part of being accountable is being a good listener and observer. You can learn much about your own behavior by observing others and listening to wise friends whom you respect. And choose wise friends to whom you can freely give an account of yourself.

What happens when there is no accountability?

GENESIS 16:6 | *Abram replied, "Look, she is your servant, so deal with her as you see fit." Then Sarai treated Hagar so harshly that she finally ran away.*

JUDGES 17:6 | *The people did whatever seemed right in their own eyes.*

Left unaccountable, people will always gravitate toward sin, the consequences of which eventually hurt them and others and pull them away from God. A wise person is grateful for being held accountable.

How can I choose the right people to hold me accountable?

1 KINGS 12:8, 10-11 | *Rehoboam rejected the advice of the older men and instead asked the opinion of the young men who had grown up with him. . . . The young men replied, "This is what you should tell those complainers: . . . 'Yes, my father laid heavy burdens on you, but I'm going to make them even heavier! My father beat you with whips, but I will beat you with scorpions!'"*

Friends are not always the best advisers, especially if their counsel is not consistent with God's Word.

1 CORINTHIANS 12:8 | *To one person the Spirit gives the ability to give wise advice; to another the same Spirit gives a message of special knowledge.*

Choose people who are especially wise and godly, who will not hesitate to help you see when you need to realign yourself with God.

PROVERBS 13:17 | *An unreliable messenger stumbles into trouble, but a reliable messenger brings healing.*

Reliability in telling the truth is critical in those holding you accountable.

How can I effectively hold someone else accountable?

EXODUS 18:21-23 | *Select from all the people some capable, honest men who fear God and hate bribes. . . . They will help you carry the load, making the task easier for you. If you follow this advice, . . . then you will be able to endure the pressures.*

Before you can help others be accountable, you must develop good judgment yourself. You must be wise, honest, and trustworthy.

Promise from God PSALM 119:9 | *How can a . . . person stay pure? By obeying your word.*

ADVERSITY

See also **PROBLEMS, WORRY**

Is God listening when I cry out because of my troubles? Does he really hear, and does he care?

PSALM 18:6 | *In my distress I cried out to the LORD; yes, I prayed to my God for help. He heard me from his sanctuary; my cry to him reached his ears.*

MATTHEW 11:28 | *Jesus said, "Come to me, all of you who are weary and carry heavy burdens, and I will give you rest."*

God's hotline is always open. There is never a busy signal, and he is never too preoccupied with anything—even managing the universe—to listen to your every need. God has both a listening ear and a caring heart.

NAHUM 1:7 | *The LORD is good, a strong refuge when trouble comes. He is close to those who trust in him.*

In most cases, the Bible doesn't say *if* trouble comes, but *when* trouble comes. No one has lived a life without some adversity.

PSALM 27:5, 7-8 | *He will conceal me . . . when troubles come; he will hide me in his sanctuary. He will place me out of reach on a high rock. . . . Hear me as I pray, O LORD. Be merciful and answer me! My heart has heard you say, "Come and talk with me." And my heart responds, "LORD, I am coming."*

Sometimes God does rescue you from adversity because of your faithfulness.

Is there any way I can avoid trouble and adversity?

JAMES 1:2-3 | *When troubles come your way, consider it an opportunity for great joy. For you know that when your faith is tested, your endurance has a chance to grow.*

Avoiding adversity may not be best for you. Though hard times may bruise you, they also can build you up and strengthen your faith.

PROVERBS 14:16 | *The wise are cautious and avoid danger; fools plunge ahead with reckless confidence.*

ROMANS 13:14 | *Clothe yourself with the presence of the Lord Jesus Christ. And don't let yourself think about ways to indulge your evil desires.*

The consequences of sin often bring unneeded adversity into your life. By obeying God's Word, you can avoid many kinds of adversity you might otherwise inflict on yourself.

PROVERBS 17:20 | *The crooked heart will not prosper; the lying tongue tumbles into trouble.*

PROVERBS 21:23 | *Watch your tongue and keep your mouth shut, and you will stay out of trouble.*

Controlling your tongue can help you avoid adversity. Many times trouble can be avoided by choosing your words wisely.

PROVERBS 11:14 | *There is safety in having many advisers.*

Following advice from wise people will help you avoid trouble.

Promise from God PSALM 46:1 | *God is our refuge and strength, always ready to help in times of trouble.*

ADVICE/ADVISERS

See also **DECISIONS, WISDOM**

Why is it important for me to get good advice?

PROVERBS 11:14 | *Without wise leadership, a nation falls; there is safety in having many advisers.*

PROVERBS 12:15 | *Fools think their own way is right, but the wise listen to others.*

PROVERBS 13:14 | *The instruction of the wise is like a life-giving fountain; those who accept it avoid the snares of death.*

PROVERBS 15:22 | *Plans go wrong for lack of advice; many advisers bring success.*

PROVERBS 19:20 | *Get all the advice and instruction you can, so you will be wise the rest of your life.*

PROVERBS 20:18 | *Plans succeed through good counsel; don't go to war without wise advice.*

Both leaders and service members need good advisers who will bring expertise, perspective, and experience to the challenges and problems they face. No one is wise enough or perceptive enough to grasp the full meaning and possibilities of a situation. The right counsel can make the difference between success or failure, prosperity or poverty, victory or defeat.

How do I evaluate the advice of others?

MATTHEW 7:16, 20 | *You can identify them by their fruit, that is, by the way they act. . . . Yes, just as you can identify a tree by its fruit, so you can identify people by their actions.*

One way to test advice is to evaluate the advisers. Do their actions match their words?

How can good advice benefit everyone?

EXODUS 18:14, 17-19 | *When Moses' father-in-law saw all that Moses was doing for the people, he asked, "What are you really accomplishing here? Why are you trying to do all this alone while everyone stands around you from morning till evening? . . . This is not good!" Moses' father-in-law exclaimed. "You're going to wear yourself out—and the people, too. This job is too heavy a burden for you to handle all by yourself. Now listen to me, and let me give you a word of advice, and may God be with you."*

Good advice can help everybody involved in a situation. The advice that Jethro, Moses' father-in-law, gave him benefited Moses and the entire nation. Moses was able to live with a more manageable load of responsibility, others were trained to participate in leadership, and the people were served in a more timely and equitable manner.

How do I give good advice to others?

PHILIPPIANS 4:8 | *Fix your thoughts on what is true, and honorable, and right, and pure, and lovely, and admirable. Think about things that are excellent and worthy of praise.*

In giving advice, make sure your motives are right—to offer the best possible advice for the situation, not to offer advice that might improve your own situation. Don't use advice as an excuse to lecture. Always have the other person's best interests in mind.

How valuable is wise advice?

PROVERBS 25:11 | *Timely advice is lovely, like golden apples in a silver basket.*

Timely advice is not merely helpful; it is essential because it comes just when you need it.

Promise from God PSALM 32:8 | *The LORD says, "I will guide you along the best pathway for your life. I will advise you and watch over you."*

AMBITION

See also **ACCOMPLISHMENTS**

When is ambition good?

PSALM 119:1-2 | *Joyful are people of integrity, who follow the instructions of the LORD. Joyful are those who obey his laws and search for him with all their hearts.*

The purest ambition of all is to pursue knowing God and to try to do what he asks.

1 THESSALONIANS 4:11-12 | *Make it your goal to live a quiet life, minding your own business and working with your hands, just as we instructed you before. Then people who are not Christians will respect the way you live.*

Ambition is good when it is directed at improving the quality of your character, not at promoting your accomplishments.

When does ambition become destructive? What is the danger of ambition?

GENESIS 11:4 | *[The people] said, "Come, let's build a great city for ourselves with a tower that reaches into the sky. This will make us famous and keep us from being scattered all over the world."*

Ambition becomes wrong when its goal is to bring glory to yourself.

MARK 10:35-37, 41 | *James and John, the sons of Zebedee, came over and spoke to [Jesus]. "Teacher," they said, "we want you to do us a favor." "What is your request?" he asked. They replied,*

"When you sit on your glorious throne, we want to sit in places of honor next to you, one on your right and the other on your left." . . . When the ten other disciples heard what James and John had asked, they were indignant.

Selfish ambition can twist your friendships into trivial competitiveness.

How can I use ambition in a positive way?

1 KINGS 8:58 | *May [the Lord] give us the desire to do his will in everything and to obey all the commands, decrees, and regulations that he gave our ancestors.*

Your motives signal whether your actions are based on selfish ambition or not. When your greatest desire is to love and serve others, then you are pursuing ambition that will affect others positively.

Promise from God PSALM 119:1-2 | *Joyful are people of integrity, who follow the instructions of the LORD. Joyful are those who obey his laws and search for him with all their hearts.*

ANGER

Why do people most often get angry?

GENESIS 4:4-5 | *The LORD accepted Abel and his gift, but he did not accept Cain and his gift. This made Cain very angry, and he looked dejected.*

NUMBERS 22:29 | *"You have made me look like a fool!" Balaam shouted.*

ESTHER 3:5 | *When Haman saw that Mordecai would not bow down or show him respect, he was filled with rage.*

Anger is often a reaction to pride being hurt. It is common for people to feel angry when they have been confronted about sinful actions, because the accused don't want others to think they are at fault.

1 SAMUEL 18:8 | *Saul [became] very angry. "What's this?" he said. "They credit David with ten thousands and me with only thousands. Next they'll be making him their king!"*

Anger is often a reaction of jealousy to what others have or to what others have accomplished.

What are the effects of anger?

GENESIS 27:41-43 | *Esau hated Jacob because their father had given Jacob the blessing. And Esau began to scheme: ". . . I will kill my brother, Jacob." But Rebekah heard about Esau's plans. So she sent for Jacob and told him, "Listen, Esau is . . . plotting to kill you. . . . Flee to my brother, Laban, in Haran."*

Anger can isolate a person from others.

PSALM 37:8 | *Stop being angry! . . . Do not lose your temper— it only leads to harm.*

JAMES 1:19-20 | *You must all be quick to listen, slow to speak, and slow to get angry. Human anger does not produce the righteousness God desires.*

Anger produces evil motives.

1 SAMUEL 20:30-31 | *Saul boiled with rage at Jonathan. . . . "As long as that son of Jesse is alive, you'll never be king. Now go and get him so I can kill him!"*

Anger blinds a person to what is really good and right. In its strongest form, anger can lead to murder.

PROVERBS 15:1 | *A gentle answer deflects anger, but harsh words make tempers flare.*

Anger leads to conflict and arguments.

When I am angry, what should I avoid?

2 CORINTHIANS 2:5-7 | *The man who caused all the trouble hurt all of you more than he hurt me. Most of you opposed him, and that was punishment enough. Now, however, it is time to forgive and comfort him. Otherwise he may be overcome by discouragement.*

EPHESIANS 6:4 | *Do not provoke your children to anger by the way you treat them.*

Avoid punishing children in the heat of anger. When a person overreacts to a situation, regrettable words and actions may result.

JAMES 3:5 | *The tongue is a small thing that makes grand speeches. But a tiny spark can set a great forest on fire.*

Avoid angrily "speaking your mind." It is bound to be something that will be regretted later.

1 SAMUEL 19:9-10 | *As David played his harp, Saul hurled his spear at David. But David dodged out of the way, and leaving the spear stuck in the wall, he fled and escaped into the night.*

Avoid acting on impulse in the heat of anger.

We all get angry at times, so what should I do about it?

EPHESIANS 4:26-27 | *"Don't sin by letting anger control you."*
Don't let the sun go down while you are still angry, for anger
gives a foothold to the devil.

Try to resolve anger quickly. Like a skunk in the house,
anger permeates all aspects of life. Don't encourage anger
to stay by feeding it. Get rid of it as soon as possible.

MATTHEW 5:21-22, 24 | *[Jesus said,] "You have heard that our*
ancestors were told, 'You must not murder. . . .' But I say, if
you are even angry with someone, you are subject to judgment!
. . . Go and be reconciled to that person."

Calmly confront those with whom you are angry in order
to restore your relationship.

1 CORINTHIANS 13:5 | *[Love] is not irritable, and it keeps no record*
of being wronged.

Love is the mightiest weapon in overcoming anger.

Promise from God PSALM 103:8 | *The LORD is compassionate*
and merciful, slow to get angry and filled with unfailing love.

AUTHORITY

Why is human authority necessary?

JUDGES 21:25 | *In those days Israel had no king; all the people*
did whatever seemed right in their own eyes.

1 PETER 2:13-14 | *For the Lord's sake, respect all human author-*
ity—whether the king as head of state, or the officials he has

*appointed. For the king has sent them to punish those who do
wrong and to honor those who do right.*

Human authority brings order and security to society. Authority in the military, the business world, and the family has the
same purpose. Properly exercised, it is essential in teaching
others, caring for others, and holding others accountable.

What if I have a bad attitude toward authority?

HEBREWS 3:7-10 | *The Holy Spirit says, "Today when you hear his
voice, don't harden your hearts as Israel did when they rebelled,
when they tested me in the wilderness. There your ancestors
tested and tried my patience, even though they saw my miracles
for forty years. So I was angry with them, and I said, 'Their
hearts always turn away from me. They refuse to do what
I tell them.'"*

Sometimes you might get tired of being told what to do;
you want to chart your own course and become your own
person. But being your own person and rebelling against
authority are two very different things. Authority is not
a bad thing—the abuse of authority is a bad thing. Being
your own person doesn't mean doing whatever you want;
it means using your God-given personality and talents to
serve him by serving others.

Is seeking to gain a position of authority a bad thing?

MATTHEW 20:26 | *Whoever wants to be a leader among you must
be your servant.*

JOHN 3:30 | *He must become greater and greater, and I must
become less and less.*

Don't seek positions of authority for the sake of power or self-promotion or blind ambition. If you want to be looked up to by others, then have a servant's heart, be willing to take responsibility for your actions (not passing the buck when it's convenient), refuse to stay silent when things are wrong, and do not seek glory for yourself. People who consistently live with integrity will be most respected and honored.

Promise from God PROVERBS 29:2 | *When the godly are in authority, the people rejoice.*

BALANCE

See also **BURNOUT, STRESS**

What is balance?

MATTHEW 22:37-40 | *Jesus replied, "'You must love the LORD your God with all your heart, all your soul, and all your mind.' This is the first and greatest commandment. A second is equally important: 'Love your neighbor as yourself.' The entire law and all the demands of the prophets are based on these two commandments."*

Balance means living a life that honors God, others, and yourself in the way you use your gifts and spend your time and resources. One of the greatest mistakes a person can make is getting out of balance by overemphasizing one aspect of his or her responsibilities at the cost of other areas.

How can I bring balance into my life?

MARK 1:35-38 | *Before daybreak the next morning, Jesus got up and went out to an isolated place to pray. Later Simon and the others went out to find him. When they found him, they said, "Everyone is looking for you." But Jesus replied, "We must go on to other towns as well, and I will preach to them, too. That is why I came."*

LUKE 5:16 | *Jesus often withdrew to the wilderness for prayer.*

Jesus modeled a life balanced by involvement and withdrawal, action and reflection, mission and meditation, effort and then time for spiritual energizing. This pace allowed him to remain open to God's direction instead of human pressures.

Promise from God ECCLESIASTES 3:1 | *For everything there is a season, a time for every activity under heaven.*

BIBLE

Is the Bible relevant today?

2 TIMOTHY 3:16 | *All Scripture is inspired by God and is useful to teach us what is true and to make us realize what is wrong in our lives. It corrects us when we are wrong and teaches us to do what is right.*

2 PETER 1:20-21 | *No prophecy in Scripture ever came from the prophet's own understanding, or from human initiative. No, those prophets were moved by the Holy Spirit, and they spoke from God.*

The Bible has stood the test of time more than any other document in human history. It has been faithfully preserved because it is God's very words to us, and he will not let them disappear from the face of the earth or be altered by human hands.

Why is the Bible worth reading?

JEREMIAH 15:16 | *When I discovered your words, I devoured them. They are my joy and my heart's delight, for I bear your name, O LORD God of Heaven's Armies.*

God's Word shapes a person's heart, mind, and soul. It brings joy and purpose to life. And it inspires those who read it to live a life that reflects God's character and leave a lasting spiritual legacy.

PSALM 119:9 | *How can a young person stay pure? By obeying your word.*

PSALM 119:11 | *I have hidden your word in my heart, that I might not sin against you.*

Reading the Bible is the way to know how to live a holy life before God.

DEUTERONOMY 17:20 | *Regular reading will prevent him from becoming proud and acting as if he is above his fellow citizens.*

Reading the Bible helps maintain a right attitude toward God and others.

PSALM 119:105 | *Your word is a lamp to guide my feet and a light for my path.*

Reading the Bible provides guidance in daily living.

PSALM 119:24 | *Your laws please me; they give me wise advice.*

PROVERBS 6:22 | *When you walk, their counsel will lead you. When you sleep, they will protect you. When you wake up, they will advise you.*

Reading the Bible offers good counsel for problems.

PSALM 119:43 | *Do not snatch your word of truth from me, for your regulations are my only hope.*

PSALM 119:50 | *Your promise revives me; it comforts me in all my troubles.*

Reading the Bible gives hope for the future.

PSALM 119:52 | *I meditate on your age-old regulations; O LORD, they comfort me.*

Reading the Bible gives great comfort.

Promise from God LUKE 11:28 | *Blessed are all who hear the word of God and put it into practice.*

BLESSINGS

How can I receive God's blessings?

EPHESIANS 1:3 | *All praise to God, the Father of our Lord Jesus Christ, who has blessed us with every spiritual blessing in the heavenly realms because we are united with Christ.*

All you are and all you have are gifts from God, to be used by him to bless others. When you truly desire to serve God, you will find yourself in the middle of a rushing stream of God's blessings, to be used to refresh others.

DEUTERONOMY 1:35-36 | *Not one of you from this wicked generation will live to see the good land I swore to give your ancestors, except Caleb. . . . He will see this land because he has followed the LORD completely.*

Throughout the Bible, you find a simple but profound principle: obeying God brings blessings, and disobeying God brings misfortune. Be careful not to think of God's blessings only in terms of material possessions—the greatest blessings are far more valuable than money or things. They come in the form of joy, family, relationships, peace of heart, spiritual gifts, and the confidence of eternal life.

What do God's blessings look like?

NUMBERS 6:24-26 | *May the LORD bless you and protect you. May the LORD smile on you and be gracious to you. May the LORD show you his favor and give you his peace.*

Like the constant movement of the ocean, God's blessings are constant, whether a person is aware of them or not. Scripture is full of blessings God gives to those who love him, including his presence, his grace, and his peace.

How can I be a blessing to others?

ROMANS 1:11-12 | *I long to visit you so I can bring you some spiritual gift that will help you grow strong in the Lord. When we get together, I want to encourage you in your faith, but I also want to be encouraged by yours.*

2 CORINTHIANS 2:14 | *Thank God! He has made us his captives and continues to lead us along in Christ's triumphal procession. Now he uses us to spread the knowledge of Christ everywhere, like a sweet perfume.*

As a person shares the blessings God has given, he or she blesses others as well.

Should I bless my enemies?

ROMANS 12:14 | *Bless those who persecute you. Don't curse them; pray that God will bless them.*

Jesus introduced a revolutionary new idea—blessing and forgiving enemies. The natural response is revenge for enemies. Praying for enemies is not an easy thing to do. But winning over enemies instead of continuing to fight with them is definitely a blessing.

Promise from God GALATIANS 6:9 | *Let's not get tired of doing what is good. At just the right time we will reap a harvest of blessing if we don't give up.*

BROKEN HEART

See also **COMFORT, GRIEF**

Does God care when my heart is broken?

PSALM 147:3 | *He heals the brokenhearted and bandages their wounds.*

God cares very much when you hurt. He feels your pain and wants to help you through your trials. It is at these times that you are often most aware of his love and comfort.

How should I respond when my heart is broken?

PSALM 61:1-2 | *O God, listen to my cry! Hear my prayer! From the ends of the earth, I cry to you for help when my heart is overwhelmed. Lead me to the towering rock of safety.*

LAMENTATIONS 1:20 | *LORD, see my anguish! My heart is broken and my soul despairs, for I have rebelled against you. In the streets the sword kills, and at home there is only death.*

It's important for a person to turn to God with hurt and ask for his help. He is the only One who can truly and fully restore what has been broken.

Promise from God PSALM 34:18 | *The LORD is close to the brokenhearted; he rescues those whose spirits are crushed.*

BURNOUT

See also **BALANCE**

How do I know if I am experiencing burnout?

PSALM 69:1-2 | *Save me, O God, for the floodwaters are up to my neck. Deeper and deeper I sink into the mire; I can't find a foothold.*

You may be experiencing burnout if your life feels over-whelming and everyday tasks seem impossible.

PROVERBS 30:1 | *I am weary, O God; I am weary and worn out, O God.*

ECCLESIASTES 2:22 | *What do people get in this life for all their hard work and anxiety?*

JEREMIAH 45:3 | *I am overwhelmed with trouble! Haven't I had enough pain already? And now the LORD has added more!*

If a person becomes exhausted and is in despair during a long stretch of work, if it seems as if work will never be done, if there is a feeling of being stuck in a rut with no way to get out, this person may be experiencing burnout.

What are some antidotes for burnout?

EXODUS 18:21-23 | *Select from all the people some capable, honest men. . . . They will help you carry the load, making the task easier for you. If you follow this advice, . . . then you will be able to endure the pressures.*

Perhaps some of the workload can be redistributed and shared by others. This can ease an individual person's burden, multiply effectiveness, and give other people the opportunity to grow.

1 KINGS 19:5-8 | *As [Elijah] was sleeping, an angel touched him and told him, "Get up and eat!" . . . So he ate and drank and lay down again. Then the angel of the LORD came again and touched him and said, "Get up and eat some more, or the journey ahead will be too much for you." So he got up and ate and drank, and the food gave him enough strength to travel forty days and forty nights to Mount Sinai, the mountain of God.*

A person needs to take good care of his or her body by exercising, resting, and eating nutritious meals. Poor nutrition and unhealthy habits invite burnout.

ISAIAH 30:15 | *Only in returning to me and resting in me will you be saved. In quietness and confidence is your strength.*

MATTHEW 11:28-29 | *Jesus said, "Come to me, all of you who are weary and carry heavy burdens, and I will give you rest. . . . And you will find rest for your souls."*

When a person experiences burnout, one consideration is to turn to the Lord for help, renewal, and refreshment.

The strength needed to persevere through life's work and difficulties comes only from God. He promises to carry a person's burdens, giving the rest needed.

Promise from God ISAIAH 40:29-31 | *He gives power to the weak and strength to the powerless. Even youths will become weak and tired, and young men will fall in exhaustion. But those who trust in the LORD will find new strength. They will soar high on wings like eagles. They will run and not grow weary. They will walk and not faint.*

CHANGE

With all the change in my life, how can I keep it all together?

LAMENTATIONS 5:19 | *LORD, you remain the same forever! Your throne continues from generation to generation.*

HEBREWS 1:12 | *You are always the same; you will live forever.*

The character of God is loving and trustworthy—and unchanging. This is good news, because no matter how much life changes, no matter what new situations are faced, God's promise to care for, help, and guide you can always be counted on.

ROMANS 8:28 | *We know that God causes everything to work together for the good of those who love God and are called according to his purpose for them.*

Sometimes change seems to be for the worse. When such change occurs, remember that traumatic, unpredictable, and unfair change never trumps God's will. No change occurs that he does not allow and that he cannot make worthwhile.

Promise from God ISAIAH 40:8 | *The grass withers and the flowers fade, but the word of our God stands forever.*

CHARACTER

See also **INTEGRITY, REPUTATION**

What are the attributes of character I should aspire to?

EZEKIEL 18:5-9 | *Suppose a certain man is righteous and does what is just and right. He does not feast in the mountains before Israel's idols or worship them. He does not commit adultery. . . . He is a merciful creditor, not keeping the items given as security by poor debtors. He does not rob the poor but instead gives food to the hungry and provides clothes for the needy. He grants loans without interest, stays away from injustice, is honest and fair when judging others, and faithfully obeys my decrees and regulations. Anyone who does these things is just and will surely live, says the Sovereign LORD.*

Justice, righteousness, mercy, honesty, fairness, faithfulness, and generosity are essential traits of an upright character.

How can I develop these character traits?

DEUTERONOMY 8:2 | *Remember how the LORD your God led you through the wilderness for these forty years, humbling you and testing you to prove your character, and to find out whether or not you would obey his commands.*

Character traits are developed through experience and testing, through getting to know God and his Word.

Promise from God ROMANS 5:4 | *Endurance develops strength of character, and character strengthens our confident hope of salvation.*

CHOICES

How do I know whether I am making good or bad choices?

GENESIS 13:10-13 | *Lot took a long look at the fertile plains of the Jordan Valley in the direction of Zoar. The whole area was well watered everywhere. . . . Lot chose for himself the whole Jordan Valley to the east of [him]. . . . Lot moved his tents to a place near Sodom and settled among the cities of the plain. But the people of this area were extremely wicked and constantly sinned against the LORD.*

GENESIS 25:30-31, 33-34 | *Esau said to Jacob, "I'm starved! Give me some of that red stew!" . . . "All right," Jacob replied, "but trade me your rights as the firstborn son.". . . So Esau swore an oath, thereby selling all his rights as the firstborn to his brother, Jacob. Then Jacob gave Esau some bread and lentil stew. Esau ate the meal, then got up and left. He showed contempt for his rights as the firstborn.*

If a person's choices are guided primarily by selfish ambition or a desire for physical fulfillment, it is very likely that they are bad choices, like the ones Lot and Esau made.

PROVERBS 12:15 | *Fools think their own way is right, but the wise listen to others.*

1 KINGS 12:8 | *But Rehoboam rejected the advice of the older men and instead asked the opinion of the younger men who had grown up with him and were now his advisers.*

If someone rejects the advice of proven wise counselors, like Rehoboam did, that person is probably making a foolish choice. But if the same person listens to advice and weighs it carefully, the better the chance that he or she will make good choices. Seek the advice of trusted friends.

PROVERBS 1:7 | *Fear of the LORD is the foundation of true knowledge, but fools despise wisdom and discipline.*

If decisions are being guided by reverence for God and by a desire for his wisdom, then a person is on the way to making good choices that will enhance his or her life.

Promise from God PSALM 23:3 | *He guides me along right paths, bringing honor to his name.*

COMFORT

See also **BROKEN HEART, GRIEF**

When does God comfort me?

PSALM 23:4 | *When I walk through the darkest valley, I will not be afraid, for you are close beside me.*

MATTHEW 5:4 | *God blesses those who mourn, for they will be comforted.*

When you grieve.

PSALM 145:14 | *The LORD helps the fallen and lifts those bent beneath their loads.*

When you are overwhelmed.

GENESIS 26:24 | *Do not be afraid, for I am with you and will bless you.*

EXODUS 14:13 | *Moses told the people, "Don't be afraid. Just stand still and watch the LORD rescue you today."*

When you are afraid.

MATTHEW 5:11 | *God blesses you when people mock you and persecute you and lie about you and say all sorts of evil things against you because you are my followers.*

When you are persecuted.

JOHN 16:33 | *Here on earth you will have many trials and sorrows. But take heart, because I have overcome the world.*

When you are suffering.

PSALM 138:3 | *As soon as I pray, you answer me; you encourage me by giving me strength.*

When you are weak and weary.

ROMANS 8:28 | *We know that God causes everything to work together for the good of those who love God and are called according to his purpose for them.*

When you worry about your future.

How does God comfort me?

PSALM 119:76 | *Let your unfailing love comfort me, just as you promised me, your servant.*

He loves you.

ROMANS 8:26 | *The Holy Spirit helps us in our weakness. For example, we don't know what God wants us to pray for. But the Holy Spirit prays for us with groanings that cannot be expressed in words.*

He prays for you.

PSALM 55:17 | *Morning, noon, and night I cry out in my distress, and the LORD hears my voice.*

He listens to you.

PSALM 94:19 | *When doubts filled my mind, your comfort gave me renewed hope and cheer.*

He gives you hope and joy.

PSALM 147:3 | *He heals the brokenhearted and bandages their wounds.*

He heals your broken heart.

How can I comfort others?

JOB 42:11 | *All [Job's] brothers, sisters, and former friends came and feasted with him in his home. And they consoled him and comforted him because of all the trials the LORD had brought against him.*

Be with them in their time of need. Just being there speaks volumes about how much a person cares.

JOB 21:2 | *Listen closely to what I am saying. That's one consolation you can give me.*

Be a good listener. It is usually more important to listen than to talk.

RUTH 2:13 | *"I hope I continue to please you, sir," she replied. "You have comforted me by speaking so kindly to me, even though I am not one of your workers."*

Speak kind and encouraging words.

PHILEMON 1:7 | *Your love has given me much joy and comfort, my brother, for your kindness has often refreshed the hearts of God's people.*

Comfort others with kind actions.

2 CORINTHIANS 1:3-4 | *All praise to God, the Father of our Lord Jesus Christ. God is our merciful Father and the source of all comfort. He comforts us in all our troubles so that we can comfort others. When they are troubled, we will be able to give them the same comfort God has given us.*

Remember the ways God has comforted you, and model that same comfort to others. When you have experienced God's assuring love, his guiding wisdom, and his sustaining power, you are able to comfort others with understanding.

Promise from God PSALM 94:19 | *When doubts filled my mind, your comfort gave me renewed hope and cheer.*

COMMITMENT

See also **LOYALTY**

Why is commitment important?

PSALM 25:10 | *The LORD leads with unfailing love and faithfulness all who keep his covenant and obey his demands.*

When you are committed to following God, God will lead you to discover his will for your life, the satisfying and fulfilling purpose for which he created you.

PSALM 31:23 | *The LORD protects those who are loyal to him.*

When you are committed to God, he is committed to watching out and caring for you.

RUTH 1:16 | *Wherever you go, I will go; wherever you live, I will live. Your people will be my people, and your God will be my God.*

Commitment is a mark of true friendship.

1 CORINTHIANS 13:7 | *Love never gives up, never loses faith, is always hopeful, and endures through every circumstance.*

Commitment to others is evidence of love for them.

What should be my most important commitments?

MATTHEW 22:37-38 | *Jesus replied, "'You must love the LORD your God with all your heart, all your soul, and all your mind.' This is the first and greatest commandment."*

To love and honor God in all you do.

GENESIS 2:24 | *A man leaves his father and mother and is joined to his wife, and the two are united into one.*

HEBREWS 13:4 | *Give honor to marriage, and remain faithful to one another in marriage. God will surely judge people who are immoral and those who commit adultery.*

To love and be devoted to your spouse.

PROVERBS 22:6 | *Direct your children onto the right path, and when they are older, they will not leave it.*

To love your children and teach them to love God.

JOHN 13:34-35 | *I am giving you a new commandment: Love each other. Just as I have loved you, you should love each other. Your love for one another will prove to the world that you are my disciples.*

To love others as God has loved you.

Promise from God HEBREWS 3:14 | *If we are faithful to the end, trusting God just as firmly as when we first believed, we will share in all that belongs to Christ.*

COMMUNICATION

See also **WORDS**

How can I best communicate with others?

2 CORINTHIANS 6:11-13 | *Oh, dear Corinthian friends! We have spoken honestly with you, and our hearts are open to you. There is no lack of love on our part, but you have withheld your love from us. I am asking you to respond as if you were my own children. Open your hearts to us!*

Confront issues tactfully but directly. If you are a leader, be committed to open, candid communication with the service members you lead and serve.

GALATIANS 6:1 | *Dear brothers and sisters, if another believer is overcome by some sin, you who are godly should gently and humbly help that person back onto the right path.*

1 THESSALONIANS 2:7 | *As apostles of Christ we certainly had a right to make some demands of you, but instead we were like children among you. Or we were like a mother feeding and caring for her own children.*

When a person is aware of a problem, it's important to get involved, being kind and gentle in the process. Those in a leadership role should pay attention and listen to the needs and struggles of those around them.

ACTS 23:1 | *Gazing intently at the high council, Paul began: "Brothers, I have always lived before God with a clear conscience!"*

Keep a clear conscience; it is your God-given internal radar to help you know right from wrong. Your interest and attention will be conveyed with your body language—especially being able to look others in the eye.

EPHESIANS 4:29 | *Don't use foul or abusive language. Let everything you say be good and helpful, so that your words will be an encouragement to those who hear them.*

COLOSSIANS 4:6 | *Let your conversation be gracious and attractive so that you will have the right response for everyone.*

Watch your language. Words should be gracious, effective, good, helpful, and encouraging to others.

PROVERBS 13:17 | *An unreliable messenger stumbles into trouble, but a reliable messenger brings healing.*

Be trustworthy and reliable.

2 CORINTHIANS 1:13 | *Our letters have been straightforward, and there is nothing written between the lines and nothing you can't understand.*

Be clear. If someone doesn't understand what is expected of him or her, take the time to explain it. That extra effort can help the person grow.

What are the side effects of poor communication?

PROVERBS 26:6 | *Trusting a fool to convey a message is like cutting off one's feet or drinking poison!*

2 TIMOTHY 2:23 | *Don't get involved in foolish, ignorant arguments that only start fights.*

JAMES 3:5-6 | *The tongue is a small thing that makes grand speeches. But a tiny spark can set a great forest on fire. And the tongue is a flame of fire. It is a whole world of wickedness, corrupting your entire body. It can set your whole life on fire, for it is set on fire by hell itself.*

Poor communication can lead to a lack of control, quarrels, evil actions, and foolishness.

Promise from God EPHESIANS 4:29 | *Let everything you say be good and helpful, so that your words will be an encouragement to those who hear them.*

COMPASSION

What can I learn about God's compassion to help me be more compassionate?

EXODUS 34:6 | *The LORD passed in front of Moses, calling out, "Yahweh! The LORD! The God of compassion and mercy! I am slow to anger and filled with unfailing love and faithfulness."*

Because God is compassionate, he is slow to get angry. Learn from him not to be quick to get angry.

PSALM 51:1 | *Have mercy on me, O God, because of your unfailing love. Because of your great compassion, blot out the stain of my sins.*

Because God is compassionate, he gives you mercy when you don't deserve it. His mercy provides what is needed to be merciful to others.

PSALM 79:8 | *Do not hold us guilty for the sins of our ancestors! Let your compassion quickly meet our needs, for we are on the brink of despair.*

Because God is compassionate, he meets your needs.

MATTHEW 14:14 | *Jesus saw the huge crowd as he stepped from the boat, and he had compassion on them and healed their sick.*

EPHESIANS 4:32 | *Be kind to each other, tenderhearted, forgiving one another, just as God through Christ has forgiven you.*

Because God is compassionate, he works in you to help you forgive others and instills a desire to want to help them.

ISAIAH 54:7 | *For a brief moment I abandoned you, but with great compassion I will take you back.*

Because God is compassionate, he wants to have a relationship with you.

Promise from God PSALM 145:9 | *The LORD is good to everyone. He showers compassion on all his creation.*

COMPETITION

Is competition good?

1 CORINTHIANS 9:24 | *Don't you realize that in a race everyone runs, but only one person gets the prize? So run to win!*

Competition can motivate a person to achieve personal improvement and to sharpen individual skills.

When does competition become a bad thing?

2 TIMOTHY 2:5 | *Athletes cannot win the prize unless they follow the rules.*

Competition is unhealthy when it causes a person to sin. If winning becomes everything, a person may be tempted to compromise his or her integrity.

LUKE 18:11 | *The Pharisee stood by himself and prayed this prayer: "I thank you, God, that I am not a sinner like everyone else. For I don't cheat, I don't sin, and I don't commit adultery. I'm certainly not like that tax collector!"*

Competition can lead to comparisons with others. This can lead to pride, and pride leads to trouble.

MATTHEW 18:1-4 | *The disciples came to Jesus and asked, "Who is greatest in the Kingdom of Heaven?" Jesus called a little child to him and put the child among them. Then he said, ... "Unless you turn from your sins and become like little children, you will never get into the Kingdom of Heaven. So anyone who becomes as humble as this little child is the greatest in the Kingdom of Heaven."*

Competition is inappropriate any time it causes you to elevate yourself above others.

People tell me I can be too competitive at times. How can I learn to lighten up?

PHILIPPIANS 2:3-4 | *Don't be selfish; don't try to impress others. Be humble, thinking of others as better than yourselves. Don't look out only for your own interests, but take an interest in others, too.*

There's nothing wrong with competing as long as you are not doing so for wrong things or out of wrong motives. Keeping a competitive nature under control keeps you from hurting someone else.

COLOSSIANS 3:23 | *Work willingly at whatever you do, as though you were working for the Lord rather than for people.*

You should strive to always do your best, rather than besting others. If besting others is your only goal, that is a sign of trying to honor yourself.

Promise from God 1 CORINTHIANS 15:57 | *Thank God! He gives us victory over sin and death through our Lord Jesus Christ.*

COMPLAINING

Is it wrong to complain?

NUMBERS 21:5-6 | *[The people] began to speak against God and Moses. "Why have you brought us out of Egypt to die here in the wilderness?" they complained. "There is nothing to eat here and nothing to drink. And we hate this horrible manna!" So the LORD sent poisonous snakes among the people, and many were bitten and died.*

Complaining is a sign of selfishness. The complainer focuses on what he or she doesn't have, and in a real sense, covets that. Complaining makes a person a negative-minded nagger.

What should I do instead of complaining?

PHILIPPIANS 2:14-15 | *Do everything without complaining and arguing, so that no one can criticize you. Live . . . as children of God, shining like bright lights in a world full of crooked and perverse people.*

Instead of complaining about others, say something positive about them. The person who can't do that shouldn't say anything at all. At least if a person is quiet, he or she can't be blamed for being negative or critical.

LAMENTATIONS 3:39-40 | *Why should we, mere humans, complain when we are punished for our sins? Instead, let us test and examine our ways. Let us turn back to the LORD.*

Instead of complaining about the wrongful things that others do, a person needs to focus on and repent of his or her own wrongdoings.

LUKE 6:37 | *Do not judge others, and you will not be judged. Do not condemn others, or it will all come back against you. Forgive others, and you will be forgiven.*

Instead of complaining about the mistakes of others, a person needs to forgive them as he or she would like to be forgiven.

Promise from God EPHESIANS 4:29 | *Let everything you say be good and helpful, so that your words will be an encouragement to those who hear them.*

CONFLICT

What causes conflict?

2 SAMUEL 15:6, 12 | *Absalom . . . stole the hearts of all the people . . . and the conspiracy gained momentum.*

JAMES 4:2 | *You want what you don't have, so you scheme and kill to get it. You are jealous of what others have, but you can't get it, so you fight and wage war to take it away from them.*

Conflict begins when a person, group, or nation isn't getting what it wants and confronts whoever or whatever is the obstacle in an effort to get it. On an individual level, a person wants someone's behavior to be different, to get his or her way on some issue, to win, to acquire someone else's possession, to gain another's loyalty. The list can go on and on. When the other person isn't willing to yield, conflict ensues. Unresolved conflict can sometimes lead to open warfare.

ACTS 15:37-39 | *Barnabas . . . wanted to take along John Mark. But Paul disagreed strongly. . . . Their disagreement was so sharp that they separated.*

Conflict begins when people with opposing viewpoints are not willing to find common ground.

ESTHER 3:2, 5-6 | *Mordecai refused to bow. . . . [Haman] was filled with rage . . . so he decided it was not enough to lay hands on Mordecai alone. . . . He looked for a way to destroy all the Jews throughout the entire empire.*

Conflict begins when a person's pride is hurt and there is a desire for revenge.

ROMANS 7:18-20 | *I know that nothing good lives in me, that is, in my sinful nature. I want to do what is right, but I can't. I want to do what is good, but I don't. I don't want to do what is wrong, but I do it anyway. . . . It is sin living in me.*

ROMANS 7:22-23 | *I love God's law with all my heart. But there is another power within me that is at war with my mind. This power makes me a slave to the sin that is still within me.*

Conflict begins when good confronts evil. The two cannot peacefully coexist, so a battle begins.

MATTHEW 23:23-24 | *[Jesus said,] "What sorrow awaits you teachers of religious law and you Pharisees. Hypocrites! For you are careful to tithe even the tiniest income from your herb gardens, but you ignore the more important aspects of the law—justice, mercy, and faith. You should tithe, yes, but do not neglect the more important things. Blind guides! You strain your water so you won't accidentally swallow a gnat, but you swallow a camel!"*

There are times when a person must not ignore certain situations and must actually initiate conflict in order to speak for truth and justice. This is healthy conflict. Jesus confronted the Pharisees not only for their hypocritical behavior but also because of their destructive influence as teachers and leaders.

What are some ways to resolve conflict?

GENESIS 13:7-9 | *Disputes broke out between the herdsmen of Abram and Lot. . . . Finally Abram said to Lot, "Let's not allow this conflict to come between us or our herdsmen. . . . Take your choice of any section of the land you want."*

Solving conflict takes initiative; someone must make the first move. Abram gave Lot first choice, putting family peace above personal desires.

GENESIS 26:21-22 | *Isaac's men then dug another well, but again there was a dispute over it. . . . Abandoning that one, Isaac moved on and dug another well. This time there was no dispute over it. . . . [Isaac] said, "At last the LORD has created enough space for us to prosper in this land."*

Solving conflict takes humility, persistence, and a preference for peace over personal victory.

2 SAMUEL 3:1 | *That was the beginning of a long war between those who were loyal to Saul and those loyal to David. As time passed David became stronger and stronger, while Saul's dynasty became weaker and weaker.*

Solving conflict involves compromise, finding common ground that is bigger than the differences between the two parties. If neither side is willing to take the initiative or show the necessary humility to seek common ground, conflict will result in a broken friendship, divorce, or even war.

JOHN 17:21 | *I pray that they will all be one, just as you and I are one—as you are in me, Father, and I am in you. And may they be in us so that the world will believe you sent me.*

Praying for peace and unity with others makes a difference because the person is seeking the help of the great Peacemaker.

How do I keep a conflict from getting out of control?

PROVERBS 17:27 | *A truly wise person uses few words; a person with understanding is even-tempered.*

Words can be used as tools or weapons and therefore must be used carefully.

MATTHEW 5:23-24 | *If you are presenting a sacrifice at the altar in the Temple and you suddenly remember that someone has something against you, leave your sacrifice there at the altar. Go and be reconciled to that person.*

Do not "bury" or deny conflicts, but rather take immediate steps to resolve them.

How can I hope to resolve conflict with an enemy?

MATTHEW 5:43-46 | *[Jesus said,] "You have heard the law that says, 'Love your neighbor' and hate your enemy. But I say, love your enemies! Pray for those who persecute you! In that way, you will be acting as true children of your Father in heaven. . . . If you love only those who love you, what reward is there for that? Even corrupt tax collectors do that much."*

Human nature wants to love friends and hate enemies. But Jesus brought a new order that adds a divine perspective— the only way to resolve some conflicts is to reach out in love to your enemy. This kind of love has sometimes eliminated enemies by turning them into friends.

Promise from God MATTHEW 5:9 | *God blesses those who work for peace, for they will be called the children of God.*

CONFRONTATION

Under what circumstances is confrontation necessary?

EPHESIANS 5:11 | *Take no part in the worthless deeds of evil and darkness; instead, expose them.*

Evil and wickedness must be confronted or they may consume a person.

2 SAMUEL 12:1, 7 | *The LORD sent Nathan the prophet to tell David this story. . . . Then Nathan said to David, "You are that man!"*

PROVERBS 27:5 | *An open rebuke is better than hidden love!*

LUKE 17:3 | *If another believer sins, rebuke that person; then if there is repentance, forgive.*

Make reconciliation the goal when confronting a wrongdoer.

How can I effectively confront others?

MATTHEW 18:15-16 | *If another believer sins against you, go privately and point out the offense. If the other person listens and confesses it, you have won that person back. But if you are unsuccessful, take one or two others with you and go back again, so that everything you say may be confirmed by two or three witnesses.*

Go to the person and confront him or her in private. If he or she does not listen, go with another concerned friend.

2 TIMOTHY 2:24 | *A servant of the Lord must not quarrel but must be kind to everyone, be able to teach, and be patient with difficult people.*

The manner of confrontation is as important as the words. It is essential to consider how you would want someone to speak to you. Confront another person in private, without quarreling or anger. Approach gently with kindness and patience. Then let God change the person's heart!

2 TIMOTHY 1:7 | *God has not given us a spirit of fear and timidity, but of power, love, and self-discipline.*

Confront others in power and love, making sure to act from a spirit that has first applied self-discipline.

How should I respond when others confront me?

PROVERBS 24:26 | *An honest answer is like a kiss of friendship.*

Receive confrontation humbly. See it as evidence that someone cares and wants what is best for you.

PROVERBS 19:25 | *If you punish a mocker, the simpleminded will learn a lesson; if you correct the wise, they will be all the wiser.*

Being confronted should increase a person's wisdom. Listen to see if you can grow wiser.

Promise from God JAMES 3:17 | *The wisdom from above is first of all pure. It is also peace loving, gentle at all times, and willing to yield to others.*

CONSCIENCE

See also **HONESTY**

Where does my conscience come from?

ROMANS 1:19-20 | *[People] know the truth about God because he has made it obvious to them. For ever since the world was created, people have seen the earth and sky. Through everything God made, they can clearly see his invisible qualities— his eternal power and divine nature. So they have no excuse for not knowing God.*

Conscience is the God-given instinct deep inside you that guides you to know right from wrong.

How does a person's conscience really work? What does it do?

GENESIS 42:21 | *[Joseph's brothers] said, "Clearly we are being punished because of what we did to Joseph long ago. We saw his anguish when he pleaded for his life, but we wouldn't listen."*

A person's conscience points out personal sin and brings a sense of guilt. It then urges action to remove this sense of guilt by righting the wrong. It is essential for a person to listen to and obey his or her conscience or it will become useless.

Can I lose my conscience?

JUDGES 17:6 | *In those days Israel had no king; all the people did whatever seemed right in their own eyes.*

PROVERBS 29:7 | *The godly care about the rights of the poor; the wicked don't care at all.*

JEREMIAH 7:24 | *[The Lord said,] "But my people would not listen to me. They kept doing whatever they wanted, following the stubborn desires of their evil hearts. They went backward instead of forward."*

MICAH 3:1-2 | *Listen, you leaders of Israel! You are supposed to know right from wrong, but you are the very ones who hate good and love evil.*

No, but a person can become so dulled to its urgings that the conscience's whisper might be dismissed or ignored. The conscience is like a muscle; it must be exercised and developed. Refusing to listen to one's conscience often makes a person feel free to do whatever he or she wants. If someone has a reputation for not always doing the right thing or is unmoved by evil or injustice, it may be an indication that the person's conscience is becoming inactive. Those who have done horrible deeds still have a conscience, but over time they have learned to tune it out, allowing them to commit those heinous deeds.

How can I develop my conscience?

HOSEA 12:6 | *Come back to your God. Act with love and justice, and always depend on him.*

Even those who have rejected God can come back to him. When a person commits to God and lives by the commands in his Word, God will restore his or her conscience.

Promise from God PSALM 119:105 | *Your word is a lamp to guide my feet and a light for my path.*

CONTENTMENT

How can I find contentment, regardless of life's circumstances?

PSALM 107:8-9 | *Let them praise the LORD for his great love and for the wonderful things he has done for them. For he satisfies the thirsty and fills the hungry with good things.*

ROMANS 8:38 | *I am convinced that nothing can ever separate us from God's love. Neither death nor life, neither angels nor demons, neither our fears for today nor our worries about tomorrow—not even the powers of hell can separate us from God's love.*

Contentment comes from the assurance that God loves you unconditionally. Nothing you do can make him love you more, and nothing you do can make him love you less.

2 CORINTHIANS 12:10 | *That's why I take pleasure in my weaknesses, and in the insults, hardships, persecutions, and troubles that I suffer for Christ. For when I am weak, then I am strong.*

PHILIPPIANS 4:11-13 | *Not that I was ever in need, for I have learned how to be content with whatever I have. I know how to live on almost nothing or with everything. I have learned the secret of living in every situation, whether it is with a full stomach or empty, with plenty or little. For I can do everything through Christ, who gives me strength.*

When contentment depends on things going your way, you become unhappy when things don't. When you watch Jesus meet your needs, the result is security and happiness because he never fails you. Jesus teaches you to discern the valuable things in life from the distractions.

MATTHEW 5:3 | *God blesses those who are poor and realize their need for him, for the Kingdom of Heaven is theirs.*

LUKE 14:33 | *You cannot become my disciple without giving up everything you own.*

Contentment comes when a person is willing to give up everything for God. Contentment is not about how much you have, but what you do for God with what you have.

GENESIS 27:41; 33:4, 9 | *Esau hated Jacob . . . and . . . began to scheme: "I will . . . kill my brother, Jacob." . . . [Later] Esau ran to meet [Jacob] and embraced him, threw his arms around his*

*neck, and kissed him. And they both wept. . . . "My brother,
I have plenty," Esau answered. "Keep what you have for yourself."*

Forgiving others is a key to contentment because it spares a
person the unhappiness that comes from holding a grudge.

What is the risk in being content?

HOSEA 13:6 | *When you had eaten and were satisfied, you became
proud and forgot [the LORD your God].*

When contentment leads to complacency, it signals trouble.
Enjoying God's blessings should lead you to stay close to him,
not forget him; to thank him, not ignore him. You are at high
risk when you find ultimate contentment in things that fail
the test of eternity—possessions, wealth, food, career, social
position—because when they fail, your contentment ends.

Promise from God PSALM 107:9 | *[The LORD] satisfies the
thirsty and fills the hungry with good things.*

COURAGE

See also **VALOR**

Where do I get the courage to go on when life seems
too hard or obstacles seem too big?

ISAIAH 41:10 | *Don't be afraid, for I am with you. Don't be
discouraged, for I am your God. I will strengthen you and
help you. I will hold you up with my victorious right hand.*

Throughout your life you will find yourself in scary situations—mortal danger, extreme stress, major illness, money

issues, or any number of problems. True courage comes from understanding that God is stronger than your strongest enemy or biggest problem, and knowing that he wants you to use his power to help you. Courage is not misplaced confidence in your own strength, but well-placed confidence in God's strength.

Will God take away the things that frighten me?

NUMBERS 14:6-7, 9 | *Two of the men who had explored the land, Joshua son of Nun and Caleb son of Jephunneh, . . . said to all the people . . . , "The land we traveled through and explored is a wonderful land! . . . Don't be afraid of the people of the land. . . . They have no protection, but the LORD is with us! Don't be afraid of them!"*

Fear is part of life and comes from feeling alone against a great threat. God may not take away things that frighten you, but he will give you courage by being beside you, helping you fight the threat. Joshua and Caleb had courage, fueled by the promise that God was greater than any enemy or problem they faced.

JOB 11:18 | *Having hope will give you courage.*

Hope helps you see beyond the immediate crisis. If God took away everything that frightened you, there would be no need for hope in your life.

Are there consequences to a lack of courage?

LUKE 23:21-24 | *[The mob] kept shouting, "Crucify him! Crucify him!" For the third time [Pilate] demanded, "Why? What crime has he committed? I have found no reason to sentence him to*

*death. So I will have him flogged, and then I will release him."
But the mob shouted louder and louder, demanding that Jesus be
crucified, and their voices prevailed. So Pilate sentenced Jesus to
die as they demanded.*

Standing up for what is right can get you in trouble with
corrupt people. Failing to stand up for what is right can get
a person in trouble with God. Pilate gave in to the demands
of corrupt people and sentenced God's Son to death.

Promise from God JOSHUA 1:9 | *Be strong and courageous!
Do not be afraid or discouraged. For the LORD your God is
with you wherever you go.*

CRISIS

What are some possible causes of crisis in my life?

JONAH 1:4, 12 | *The LORD hurled a powerful wind over the
sea, causing a violent storm that threatened to break the ship
apart. . . . "Throw me into the sea," Jonah said, "and it will
become calm again. I know that this terrible storm is all
my fault."*

Jonah was in crisis because he ran away from God, but the
sailors were in crisis, too, because of Jonah's sin! A person's
crisis may be caused by his or her own sin or someone else's.

PROVERBS 27:12 | *A prudent person foresees danger and takes
precautions. The simpleton goes blindly on and suffers the
consequences.*

Sometimes a crisis is the result of poor decisions.

ECCLESIASTES 9:12 | *People can never predict when hard times might come. Like fish in a net or birds in a trap, people are caught by sudden tragedy.*

Sometimes a crisis comes for no apparent reason. It's no one's fault—just a part of living in this world.

JOB 36:15 | *By means of their suffering, [God] rescues those who suffer. For he gets their attention through adversity.*

Sometimes God allows a crisis in your life to get your attention.

Can blessings come from my times of crisis?

JONAH 1:16 | *The sailors were awestruck by the LORD's great power, and they offered him a sacrifice and vowed to serve him.*

Sometimes a crisis helps you see God more clearly.

ROMANS 5:3-4 | *We can rejoice, too, when we run into problems and trials, for we know that they help us develop endurance. And endurance develops strength of character, and character strengthens our confident hope of salvation.*

Times of crisis can strengthen your character.

How should I respond to crisis?

PSALM 57:1 | *Have mercy on me, O God, have mercy! I look to you for protection. I will hide beneath the shadow of your wings until the danger passes by.*

PSALM 130:1-2 | *From the depths of despair, O LORD, I call for your help. Hear my cry, O Lord. Pay attention to my prayer.*

When you reach the end of your rope, call upon the Lord. Your times of weakness are times to discover his strength; your crises are his opportunities.

PSALM 119:143 | *As pressure and stress bear down on me, I find joy in your commands.*

When a crisis threatens to overwhelm you, consider reading God's Word.

Promise from God PSALM 46:1 | *God is our refuge and strength, always ready to help in times of trouble.*

CRITICISM

How should I respond to criticism? How do I evaluate whether it is constructive or destructive?

PROVERBS 12:16-18 | *A wise person stays calm when insulted. An honest witness tells the truth; a false witness tells lies. Some people make cutting remarks, but the words of the wise bring healing.*

Stay calm and don't lash back. Measure criticism according to the character of the person who is giving it. Ask yourself if the criticism is meant to heal or hurt.

1 CORINTHIANS 4:4 | *My conscience is clear, but that doesn't prove I'm right. It is the Lord himself who will examine me and decide.*

Always work to maintain a clear conscience by being honest and trustworthy. This allows you to shrug off criticism you know is unjustified.

PROVERBS 15:31-32 | *If you listen to constructive criticism, you will be at home among the wise. If you reject discipline, you only harm yourself; but if you listen to correction, you grow in understanding.*

Don't reject truthful information that will help you grow. This requires a great deal of humility because accepting criticism is a hard thing to do. Sometimes it's painful to hear the truth, but it's worse to continue harmful behavior.

PROVERBS 15:1 | *A gentle answer deflects anger, but harsh words make tempers flare.*

When unjustly criticized, respond gently with the truth. Getting angry and defensive will only make the criticism seem true.

How do I offer criticism appropriately?

JOHN 8:7 | *Let the one who has never sinned throw the first stone!*

ROMANS 2:1 | *When you say they are wicked and should be punished, you are condemning yourself, for you who judge others do these very same things.*

Before criticizing another person, take an inventory of your own shortcomings so that you can approach the person with understanding and humility.

1 CORINTHIANS 13:5 | *[Love] does not demand its own way. It is not irritable, and it keeps no record of being wronged.*

Constructive criticism is always offered in love, with the motivation to build the other person up. It addresses a specific need in someone else, not a list of his or her shortcomings or character flaws.

Promise from God   ROMANS 14:17-18 | *The Kingdom of God is . . . living a life of goodness and peace and joy in the Holy Spirit. If you serve Christ with this attitude, you will please God, and others will approve of you, too.*

DECISIONS

See also **ADVICE/ADVISERS**

What are some principles of good decision making?

PROVERBS 18:13 | *Spouting off before listening to the facts is both shameful and foolish.*

Make sure you have all the facts.

PROVERBS 18:15 | *Intelligent people are always ready to learn. Their ears are open for knowledge.*

Be open to ideas.

PROVERBS 12:15 | *Fools think their own way is right, but the wise listen to others.*

Seek the advice of trusted friends.

MATTHEW 16:26 | *What do you benefit if you gain the whole world but lose your own soul? Is anything worth more than your soul?*

Resist the temptation to make choices guided by a desire for personal satisfaction. Such ambition will lead you to make some very bad decisions.

Promise from God   JAMES 1:5 | *If you need wisdom, ask our generous God, and he will give it to you. He will not rebuke you for asking.*

DELEGATION

See also **LEADERSHIP, TEAMWORK**

Why is delegation important?

EXODUS 18:14, 18, 21-22 | *When Moses' father-in-law saw all that Moses was doing for the people, he asked, "What are you really accomplishing here? Why are you trying to do all this alone? . . . You're going to wear yourself out—and the people, too. This job is too heavy a burden for you to handle all by yourself. . . . But select from all the people some capable, honest men who fear God and hate bribes. Appoint them as leaders over groups of one thousand, one hundred, fifty, and ten. They should always be available to solve the people's common disputes, but have them bring the major cases to you."*

Delegation is necessary for all who are involved: for leaders, for those who serve with the leader, and for those who are being served. Without delegation, you will be over-burdened, the helpers under-utilized, and the people under-served. Delegation is not laziness but wise use of everyone's resources and time.

How do I delegate?

MATTHEW 10:1, 5 | *Jesus called his twelve disciples together and gave them authority to cast out evil spirits and to heal every kind of disease and illness. . . . Jesus sent out the twelve apostles with these instructions.*

Delegation is not simply letting go of work or "dumping" things you don't want to do on others. Delegation is a form of discipleship. After the disciples had spent some time with Jesus, he delegated his ministry in an initial way to these followers. He gave them specific instructions, trusted them, and valued their contribution.

2 TIMOTHY 2:2 | *Teach these truths to other trustworthy people who will be able to pass them on to others.*

Delegation develops others who, in turn, can develop still others. You should care as much about helping others learn and accomplish as you care about your own accomplishments. Delegation is a primary strategy for nurturing maturity and responsibility in those you lead.

Promise from God 1 CORINTHIANS 12:11 | *It is the one and only Spirit who distributes all these gifts. He alone decides which gift each person should have.*

DESIRES

Is it okay to want something?

1 KINGS 3:5 | *The LORD appeared to Solomon in a dream, and God said, "What do you want? Ask, and I will give it to you!"*

PROVERBS 13:12 | *Hope deferred makes the heart sick, but a dream fulfilled is a tree of life.*

God created desire within you as a means of expressing yourself. Desire is good and healthy if directed toward the proper object: that which is good and right and God-honoring. It is ironic that a desire can be right or wrong, depending upon your motive and the object of your desire. The desire to lead is healthy if your motive is to serve others, but unhealthy and wrong if your motive is to gain power to control others.

PHILIPPIANS 4:8 | *Fix your thoughts on what is true, and honorable, and right, and pure, and lovely, and admirable. Think about things that are excellent and worthy of praise.*

Desiring sin is always wrong. Make sure the object of your desire is good and helpful to others.

How do I resist evil desires?

JAMES 3:13 | *If you are wise and understand God's ways, prove it by living an honorable life, doing good works with the humility that comes from wisdom.*

Keep yourself busy with good deeds.

MATTHEW 6:13 | *Don't let us yield to temptation, but rescue us from the evil one.*

Pray that good desires will overcome bad ones.

2 CHRONICLES 34:33 | *Josiah removed all detestable idols from the entire land.*

Take away the source of temptation.

PROVERBS 15:22 | *Plans go wrong for lack of advice; many advisers bring success.*

Find a person willing to help you. You (and everyone else) need someone who will encourage you and hold you accountable.

Can God help me change the desires within my heart? How?

ROMANS 7:6 | *We can serve God, not in the old way . . . but in the new way of living in the Spirit.*

When you give control of your life to God, he gives you a new heart, a new nature, and a new desire to please him.

EZRA 1:5 | *God stirred the hearts of the priests and Levites . . . to go to Jerusalem to rebuild the Temple of the LORD.*

God stirs your heart with right desires. It is up to you to ask him for help to act upon them.

Promise from God EZEKIEL 36:26 | *[The Sovereign LORD said,] "I will give you a new heart, and I will put a new spirit in you. I will take out your stony, stubborn heart and give you a tender, responsive heart."*

DIFFERENCES

See also **PREJUDICE**

How does God want me to handle differences with others?

PSALM 133:1-3 | *How wonderful and pleasant it is when brothers live together in harmony! For harmony is as precious as the anointing oil. . . . Harmony is as refreshing as the dew. . . . The LORD has pronounced his blessing, even life everlasting.*

Live in harmony despite your differences.

PROVERBS 17:14 | *Starting a quarrel is like opening a floodgate, so stop before a dispute breaks out.*

1 CORINTHIANS 1:10 | *I appeal to you, dear brothers and sisters, by the authority of our Lord Jesus Christ, to live in harmony with each other. Let there be no divisions in the church. Rather, be of one mind, united in thought and purpose.*

Arguing over differences of opinion usually does more harm than good. Instead, talk about how your differences can become part of the solution. This helps everyone be more productive, and it promotes peace.

Can my differences with others help me be stronger?

PROVERBS 27:17 | *As iron sharpens iron, so a friend sharpens a friend.*

ROMANS 12:5 | *So it is with Christ's body. We are many parts of one body, and we all belong to each other.*

People with different gifts and perspectives make any group stronger. Ironically, it is usually through diversity that the most progress is made. If everyone always thought the same way, the status quo would never change and little would get done.

Promise from God 2 CORINTHIANS 13:11 | *Live in harmony and peace. Then the God of love and peace will be with you.*

DISCOURAGEMENT

How can I recover from discouragement?

1 KINGS 19:10 | *[Elijah said,] "I am the only one left, and now they are trying to kill me, too."*

PSALM 25:16-18 | *Turn to me and have mercy, for I am alone and in deep distress. My problems go from bad to worse. Oh, save me from them all! Feel my pain and see my trouble. Forgive all my sins.*

1 PETER 5:8-9 | *Watch out for your great enemy, the devil. He prowls around like a roaring lion, looking for someone to devour. Stand firm against him, and be strong in your faith. Remember that your Christian brothers and sisters all over the world are going through the same kind of suffering you are.*

When you are discouraged, there is a tendency to feel sorry for yourself. This feeling often becomes addicting because self-pity inexplicably feels good. However, don't let it get a hold on you, for it leads down a path to depression and destruction. Guard against thinking you are the only one who is going through troubles—it is encouraging to realize others are going through similar trials.

PSALM 55:22 | *Give your burdens to the LORD, and he will take care of you.*

PSALM 142:3 | *When I am overwhelmed, you alone know the way I should turn.*

MATTHEW 11:28 | *Jesus said, "Come to me, all of you who are weary and carry heavy burdens, and I will give you rest."*

Let God carry your burdens when they are too heavy. This doesn't mean he will take all your problems away or that he will solve your problems immediately. But for now, God promises to give you wisdom, strength, comfort, and discernment to help you.

NEHEMIAH 4:10, 14 | *The people of Judah began to complain, "The workers are getting tired, and there is so much rubble to be moved. We will never be able to build the wall by ourselves." . . . As I looked over the situation, I called together the . . . people and said to them, "Don't be afraid of the enemy! Remember the Lord, who is great and glorious, and fight for your brothers, your sons, your daughters, your wives, and your homes!"*

ROMANS 12:6 | *God has given us different gifts for doing certain things well.*

1 CORINTHIANS 15:58 | *Be strong and immovable. Always work enthusiastically for the Lord, for you know that nothing you do for the Lord is ever useless.*

GALATIANS 6:9 | *Let's not get tired of doing what is good. At just the right time we will reap a harvest of blessing if we don't give up.*

When you are discouraged, try to remember the things you are passionate about. Why do you have these passions? You might not know at the time how you will use them, but God gave you gifts and interests for a reason. Knowing this—and knowing that the more involved you are with your passions, the more fulfilled you will be—will give you encouragement.

How can I get past my insecurity and accept myself?

PSALM 8:4-5 | *What are mere mortals that you should think about them, human beings that you should care for them? Yet you made them only a little lower than God and crowned them with glory and honor.*

PSALM 139:17 | *How precious are your thoughts about me, O God. They cannot be numbered!*

MATTHEW 10:29-31 | *What is the price of two sparrows—one copper coin? But not a single sparrow can fall to the ground without your Father knowing it. And the very hairs on your head are all numbered. So don't be afraid; you are more valuable to God than a whole flock of sparrows.*

Remind yourself how valuable you are to God. He made you just as you are for a specific purpose.

PROVERBS 15:22 | *Plans go wrong for lack of advice; many advisers bring success.*

PROVERBS 19:20 | *Get all the advice and instruction you can, so you will be wise the rest of your life.*

PROVERBS 27:9 | *The heartfelt counsel of a friend is as sweet as perfume and incense.*

Get help if you can't seem to get on top of your insecurity. There is a certain healing that comes to you when you share your troubles with others.

Promise from God NEHEMIAH 8:10 | *Don't be dejected and sad, for the joy of the LORD is your strength!*

DUTY

See also **HONOR, RESPONSIBILITY**

Why is a sense of duty an important character trait?

GENESIS 39:2-3 | *The LORD was with Joseph, so he succeeded in everything he did as he served in the home of his Egyptian master. Potiphar noticed this and realized that the LORD was with Joseph, giving him success in everything he did.*

GENESIS 41:41 | *Pharaoh said to Joseph, "I hereby put you in charge of the entire land of Egypt."*

Duty can open doors of opportunity. If you are responsible with what you are given, greater opportunities and more responsibility will come your way.

GALATIANS 6:5 | *We are each responsible for our own conduct.*

Duty is important because you will be held accountable for your own actions. You cannot blame others for what you choose to do.

What are some things for which I am responsible, other than the requirements of my job?

GENESIS 2:15 | *The LORD God placed the man in the Garden of Eden to tend and watch over it.*

PSALM 8:4-6 | *What are mere mortals that you should think about them . . . ? Yet you made them only a little lower than God. . . . You gave them charge of everything you made, putting all things under their authority.*

You are responsible for the care of God's creation.

GENESIS 43:8-9 | *Judah said to his father, "Send the boy with me, and we will be on our way. . . . I personally guarantee his safety. You may hold me responsible if I don't bring him back to you."*

You are responsible for keeping your promises.

EXODUS 21:18-19 | *Now suppose two men quarrel, and one hits the other with a stone or fist, and the injured person does not die but is confined to bed. If he is later able to walk outside again, even with a crutch, the assailant will not be punished but must compensate his victim for lost wages and provide for his full recovery.*

You are responsible to compensate others for any injury or harm you cause them.

MATTHEW 12:37 | *The words you say will either acquit you or condemn you.*

You are responsible for the words you speak.

1 KINGS 1:6 | *His father, King David, had never disciplined him at any time, even by asking, "Why are you doing that?"*

You are responsible for disciplining your children.

Promise from God   MATTHEW 25:29 | *To those who use well what they are given, even more will be given, and they will have an abundance. But from those who do nothing, even what little they have will be taken away.*

ENCOURAGEMENT

How can I be an encouragement to others?

1 SAMUEL 23:16 | *Jonathan went to find David and encouraged him to stay strong in his faith in God.*

Through your words and example you can inspire others.

EZRA 5:1-2 | *Haggai and Zechariah . . . prophesied to the Jews in Judah and Jerusalem. . . . Zerubbabel . . . responded by starting again to rebuild the Temple of God in Jerusalem. And the prophets of God were with them and helped them.*

Sometimes encouragement means getting a person involved once again in productive work.

PHILEMON 1:11 | *He is very useful to both of us.*

Tell others how valuable they are to you.

JOB 29:24 | *When they were discouraged, I smiled at them. My look of approval was precious to them.*

PROVERBS 15:30 | *A cheerful look brings joy to the heart; good news makes for good health.*

Sometimes something as simple as a look that communicates approval and acceptance is a great encouragement.

HEBREWS 10:24 | *Think of ways to motivate one another to acts of love and good works.*

We can build one another up by regular, intentional affirmations.

1 THESSALONIANS 5:11 | *Encourage each other and build each other up, just as you are already doing.*

EPHESIANS 4:29 | *Don't use foul or abusive language. Let everything you say be good and helpful, so that your words will be an encouragement to those who hear them.*

We can think before we speak, choosing our words carefully.

How does God encourage me?

MATTHEW 9:22 | *Jesus . . . said, "Daughter, be encouraged! Your faith has made you well." And the woman was healed at that moment.*

He heals you and renews your faith.

PSALM 138:3 | *As soon as I pray, you answer me; you encourage me by giving me strength.*

God responds when you talk to him and gives you strength when you are weak.

HEBREWS 12:5 | *Have you forgotten the encouraging words God spoke to you as his children? He said, "My child, don't make light of the LORD's discipline, and don't give up when he corrects you."*

Be encouraged that God loves you enough to correct you and keep you on the best path for your life.

Promise from God 2 CORINTHIANS 13:11 | *Be joyful. Grow to maturity. Encourage each other. Live in harmony and peace. Then the God of love and peace will be with you.*

ENDURANCE

See also **PERSONAL DISCIPLINE**

What are the benefits of endurance?

PSALM 119:147-148 | *I rise early, before the sun is up; I cry out for help and put my hope in your words. I stay awake through the night, thinking about your promise.*

PSALM 17:5 | *My steps have stayed on your path; I have not wavered from following you.*

It helps you recommit to a plan. When you are in the midst of a difficult situation or have a goal that seems unreachable, digging deep gives you fortitude for anything that comes your way.

1 CORINTHIANS 4:12 | *We work wearily with our own hands to earn our living. We bless those who curse us. We are patient with those who abuse us.*

It will help you deal with difficult people. You must endure with kindness and patience as you deal with people who make life tough on you. This is the only way to win them over, by patiently pouring on them the love of Christ.

ACTS 14:22 | *They encouraged them to continue in the faith, reminding them that we must suffer many hardships to enter the Kingdom of God.*

It will empower you in life's most trying moments. Each one of us will experience some degree of hardship in life, whether it be suffering through persecutions, trials, or tribulations. Endurance through such times demonstrates that your faith is strong and real and can withstand any difficult test.

GALATIANS 6:9 | *Let's not get tired of doing what is good. At just the right time we will reap a harvest of blessing if we don't give up.*

It will motivate you to be on the lookout for ways to make a difference. It is difficult to do good over a long period of time when life continually throws you curveballs. An enduring faith, however, is up to the challenge.

2 PETER 1:5-6 | *Make every effort to respond to God's promises. Supplement your faith with a generous provision of moral excellence, and moral excellence with knowledge, and knowledge with self-control, and self-control with patient endurance, and patient endurance with godliness.*

It strengthens all aspects of your character. Endurance is like the fire that purifies precious metals and hardens valuable pottery. It cleanses, clarifies, and solidifies core values.

How do I develop endurance?

ROMANS 15:5 | *May God, who gives this patience and encouragement, help you live in complete harmony with each other, as is fitting for followers of Christ Jesus.*

EPHESIANS 6:13 | *Put on every piece of God's armor so you will be able to resist the enemy in the time of evil. Then after the battle you will still be standing firm.*

Endurance originates with God. He is your source of the power and perseverance you need to endure.

ROMANS 5:3 | *We can rejoice, too, when we run into problems and trials, for we know that they help us develop endurance.*

Of course you don't like problems, trials, troubles, and the testing of your faith, for they can drag you down. But they can also lift you up, and when they do, you have learned endurance.

Promise from God JAMES 1:2-4 | *When troubles come your way, consider it an opportunity for great joy. For you know that when your faith is tested, your endurance has a chance to grow. So let it grow, for when your endurance is fully developed, you will be perfect and complete, needing nothing.*

ENEMIES

What does it mean to love my enemies?

MATTHEW 5:43-44 | *[Jesus said,] "You have heard the law that says, 'Love your neighbor' and hate your enemy. But I say, love your enemies! Pray for those who persecute you!"*

ROMANS 12:20-21 | *If your enemies are hungry, feed them. If they are thirsty, give them something to drink. In doing this, you will heap burning coals of shame on their heads. Don't let evil conquer you, but conquer evil by doing good.*

Loving your enemies is always unreasonable—unless you realize that all of us were enemies of God until he forgave us. When you love an enemy, you see him or her as Christ does—a person in need of grace. Getting to that point takes prayer. You can't pray for people and not feel compassion for them.

MATTHEW 18:21-22 | *Peter . . . asked, "Lord, how often should I forgive someone who sins against me? Seven times?" "No, not seven times," Jesus replied, "but seventy times seven!"*

Respond to your enemies with forgiveness—no matter what they try to do.

Is it possible to turn an enemy into a friend?

1 PETER 2:12 | *Be careful to live properly among your unbelieving neighbors. Then even if they accuse you of doing wrong, they will see your honorable behavior.*

There is nothing more powerful and effective than an enemy who has become a friend. With love, forgiveness, prayer, and kind words, you will be able to turn some of your enemies into your friends.

Promise from God 2 THESSALONIANS 3:3 | *The Lord is faithful; he will strengthen you and guard you from the evil one.*

EXAMPLE

In what ways can I be a good example?

JEREMIAH 1:10 | *[The Lord said,] "Today I appoint you to stand up against nations and kingdoms."*

A good role model not only does what is right but speaks out against wrong.

1 THESSALONIANS 1:5 | *You know of our concern for you from the way we lived when we were with you.*

A good role model is responsible and accountable and shows those traits by actions.

MATTHEW 5:13 | *You are the salt of the earth. But what good is salt if it has lost its flavor?*

TITUS 2:7 | *You . . . must be an example . . . by doing good works of every kind. Let everything you do reflect the integrity and seriousness of your teaching.*

A good role model is not influenced by evil but rather does good to others and also influences others for good.

HOSEA 6:3 | *Oh, that we might know the LORD! Let us press on to know him.*

Being a good role model doesn't mean that you are perfect but that you are striving for maturity.

MATTHEW 20:28 | *Even the Son of Man came not to be served but to serve others and to give his life as a ransom for many.*

Being a good role model doesn't make you a celebrity; it makes you a servant.

1 TIMOTHY 4:12 | *Don't let anyone think less of you because you are young. Be an example to all believers in what you say, in the way you live, in your love, your faith, and your purity.*

Age need not be a barrier to being a good role model.

Promise from God HEBREWS 12:12-13 | *Take a new grip with your tired hands and strengthen your weak knees. Mark out a straight path for your feet so that those who are weak and lame will not fall but become strong.*

EXCELLENCE

Where did the concept of excellent workmanship originate?

GENESIS 1:31 | *God looked over all he had made, and he saw that it was very good!*

PSALM 19:1 | *The heavens proclaim the glory of God. The skies display his craftsmanship.*

The splendor of pristine creation—nature, animals, and people—was excellence in its purest form. Not only was the end product excellent, but it was excellent in every detail. The glory of the Creator was reflected in the excellence of his creation.

ISAIAH 35:2 | *Yes, there will be an abundance of flowers and singing and joy! The deserts will become as green as the mountains of Lebanon, as lovely as Mount Carmel or the plain of Sharon. There the LORD will display his glory, the splendor of our God.*

All nature sings and displays a beauty of symmetry that surpasses all the finest musical, poetic, or artistic genius of all people anytime, anywhere.

Why should I strive to be excellent?

1 CHRONICLES 26:6 | *Shemaiah had sons with great ability who earned positions of great authority.*

Excellence is highly valued. Those who strive for excellence are often promoted to significant positions in order to impact a greater number of people.

2 CHRONICLES 30:21-22, 26 | *Each day the Levites and priests sang to the LORD, accompanied by loud instruments. Hezekiah encouraged all the Levites regarding the skill they displayed. . . . There was great joy in the city, for Jerusalem had not seen a celebration like this one since the days of Solomon, King David's son.*

Excellence is appreciated. It inspires, satisfies, blesses, and motivates others.

NEHEMIAH 13:13 | *These men had an excellent reputation, and it was their job to make honest distributions to their fellow Levites.*

Excellence usually enhances your reputation.

PROVERBS 12:24 | *Work hard and become a leader.*

Excellence engages and challenges you; it urges you to make a unique contribution.

1 PETER 4:11 | *Do you have the gift of helping others? Do it with all the strength and energy that God supplies.*

Excellence is helpful to others.

Promise from God COLOSSIANS 3:23 | *Work willingly at whatever you do, as though you were working for the Lord rather than for people.*

FAILURE

How can I avoid failure?

JOSHUA 8:1 | *The LORD said to Joshua, "Do not be afraid or discouraged."*

Giving up is a sure way to fail. Courage and perseverance help prevent failure.

ISAIAH 42:23 | *Who will hear these lessons from the past and see the ruin that awaits you in the future?*

You can avoid failure by learning from the mistakes of the past.

PROVERBS 15:22 | *Plans go wrong for lack of advice; many advisers bring success.*

Good advice helps prevent failure. A concert of wise counsel makes good music for success.

What must I learn about failure?

GENESIS 3:12-13 | *The man replied, "It was the woman you gave me who gave me the fruit, and I ate it." Then the LORD God asked the woman, "What have you done?" "The serpent deceived me," she replied.*

One thing is certain: You must learn to live with failure. Everyone has weaknesses. The key is not how seldom you fail but how you respond to failure. Adam and Eve, for example, responded to their failure by trying to place the blame elsewhere rather than admitting their wrongs and seeking forgiveness.

COLOSSIANS 3:23-24 | *Work willingly at whatever you do, as though you were working for the Lord rather than for people. Remember that the Lord will give you an inheritance as your reward, and that the Master you are serving is Christ.*

If you define success in terms of faithfulness to God, he will reward your faithfulness even if you fail in the eyes of the world.

Promise from God PSALM 37:23-24 | *The LORD directs the steps of the godly. He delights in every detail of their lives. Though they stumble, they will never fall, for the LORD holds them by the hand.*

FAIRNESS

Why is fairness important?

EXODUS 23:2-3 | *You must not follow the crowd in doing wrong. When you are called to testify in a dispute, do not be swayed by the crowd to twist justice. And do not slant your testimony in favor of a person just because that person is poor.*

LEVITICUS 19:15 | *Do not twist justice in legal matters by favoring the poor or being partial to the rich and powerful. Always judge people fairly.*

Fairness means treating people equally, as much as possible, and to refrain from judging them with preset opinions.

ISAIAH 33:15-16 | *Those who are honest and fair, who refuse to profit by fraud, who stay far away from bribes, who refuse to listen to those who plot murder, who shut their eyes to all enticement to do wrong—these are the ones who will dwell on high.*

JEREMIAH 22:3 | *This is what the LORD says: Be fair-minded and just. Do what is right! Help those who have been robbed; rescue them from their oppressors.*

When the opportunity presents itself, work for justice and fairness for others.

How should I respond when life isn't fair?

ECCLESIASTES 9:11 | *The fastest runner doesn't always win the race, and the strongest warrior doesn't always win the battle. The wise sometimes go hungry, and the skillful are not necessarily wealthy.*

It is true that life is not always fair. Things don't necessarily happen the way you expect. But if you look around, you will realize that many other people are worse off than you are, so you have much to be grateful for.

EZEKIEL 18:25 | *[The Lord said,] "You say, 'The LORD isn't doing what's right!' Listen to me, O people of Israel. Am I the one not doing what's right, or is it you?"*

Don't blame God for the unfairness of other people.

PSALM 9:8 | *He will judge the world with justice and rule the nations with fairness.*

ISAIAH 9:7 | *His government and its peace will never end. He will rule with fairness and justice from the throne of his ancestor David for all eternity.*

Recognize that right will ultimately triumph, when God takes command and rules with justice and fairness forever.

Promise from God PSALM 37:28 | *The LORD loves justice, and he will never abandon the godly. He will keep them safe forever.*

FAREWELLS

What will help me say good-bye in a positive way?

ACTS 20:36-38 | *When he had finished speaking, he knelt and prayed with them. They all cried as they embraced and kissed him good-bye. They were sad most of all because he had said that they would never see him again.*

Being open and honest about the pain of parting is important to healthy good-byes.

PHILEMON 1:7 | *Your love has given me much joy and comfort, my brother, for your kindness has often refreshed the hearts of God's people.*

Before parting, thank people for what they have meant to you.

ACTS 20:32 | *Now I entrust you to God and the message of his grace that is able to build you up and give you an inheritance with all those he has set apart for himself.*

Believe that God will take care of those to whom you say farewell. God is near to those with whom you are far apart. There is great comfort in that truth.

Promise from God   MATTHEW 28:20 | *Be sure of this: I am with you always, even to the end of the age.*

FEAR

What can I do when I am overcome with fear?

DEUTERONOMY 31:6 | *Be strong and courageous! Do not be afraid and do not panic. . . . For the LORD your God will personally go ahead of you. He will neither fail you nor abandon you.*

JOHN 14:27 | *[Jesus said,] "I am leaving you with a gift—peace of mind and heart. And the peace I give is a gift the world cannot give. So don't be troubled or afraid."*

Remind yourself that God is always with you. Your situation may be genuinely threatening, but God has not abandoned you and he promises to stay with you. Even if your situation is so bad that it results in death, God has not left you but has instead ushered you into his very presence.

2 TIMOTHY 1:7 | *God has not given us a spirit of fear and timidity, but of power, love, and self-discipline.*

Whatever makes you afraid is an opportunity for you to develop greater faith as you call upon the power of God to help you.

GENESIS 26:7 | *He was afraid to say, "She is my wife." He thought, "They will kill me to get her."*

JOSHUA 17:16 | *The Canaanites . . . have iron chariots. . . . They are too strong for us.*

Fear must not keep you from doing the things you know are right. You are not meant to live in fear.

Promise from God ISAIAH 41:10 | *Don't be afraid, for I am with you. Don't be discouraged, for I am your God. I will strengthen you and help you. I will hold you up with my victorious right hand.*

FOCUS

See also **VISION**

How do I remain focused amid distractions?

HEBREWS 12:13 | *Mark out a straight path for your feet so that those who are weak and lame will not fall but become strong.*

Make clear goals and then follow those goals without wavering.

ACTS 6:3-4 | *Select seven men who are well respected and are full of the Spirit and wisdom. We will give them this responsibility [of the daily food distribution]. Then we apostles can spend our time in prayer and teaching the word.*

Stay focused on what you do well, and learn to delegate to others tasks they can do as well as or better than you.

PSALM 119:157 | *Many persecute and trouble me, yet I have not swerved from your laws.*

DANIEL 6:13 | *[The officials] told the king, "That man Daniel, one of the captives from Judah, is ignoring you and your law. He still prays to his God three times a day."*

Don't let anything distract you from what you know you should be doing or what you know is right.

PHILIPPIANS 3:13 | *I focus on this one thing: Forgetting the past and looking forward to what lies ahead.*

Don't let your past drag you down; that can be very distracting.

Promise from God HEBREWS 12:1-2 | *Let us strip off every weight that slows us down, especially the sin that so easily trips us up. And let us run with endurance the race God has set before us. We do this by keeping our eyes on Jesus.*

FORGIVENESS

See also **REGRETS**

What does it really mean to be forgiven?

ISAIAH 1:18 | *The LORD [said,] "Though your sins are like scarlet, I will make them as white as snow. Though they are red like crimson, I will make them as white as wool."*

COLOSSIANS 1:22 | *You are holy and blameless as you stand before him without a single fault.*

Forgiveness means that God looks at you as though you had never sinned. When you receive his forgiveness, you are blameless before him. When God forgives, he doesn't sweep your sins under the carpet; instead, he completely washes them away.

MATTHEW 5:44 | *Love your enemies! Pray for those who persecute you!*

Forgiveness paves the way for harmonious relationships, even with your enemies.

ROMANS 6:6 | *Our old sinful selves were crucified with Christ so that sin might lose its power in our lives. We are no longer slaves to sin.*

COLOSSIANS 2:13 | *You were dead because of your sins and because your sinful nature was not yet cut away. Then God made you alive with Christ, for he forgave all our sins.*

Forgiveness brings great joy because you are no longer a captive to your sinful nature.

ACTS 2:38 | *Each of you must repent of your sins and turn to God, and be baptized in the name of Jesus Christ for the forgiveness of your sins. Then you will receive the gift of the Holy Spirit.*

Forgiveness of sins allows you to receive the gift of God's Holy Spirit. The Holy Spirit allows you to tap into the very power of God to help you battle temptation and to guide you through life.

Can any sin be forgiven?

JOEL 2:32 | *Everyone who calls on the name of the LORD will be saved.*

MARK 3:28 | *[Jesus said,] "I tell you the truth, all sin . . . can be forgiven."*

ROMANS 8:38 | *Nothing can ever separate us from God's love.*

Forgiveness is not based on the magnitude of the sin but on the magnitude of the forgiver's love. No sin is too great for God's complete and unconditional love. The Bible does actually mention one unforgivable sin—an attitude of defiant hostility toward God that prevents us from accepting his forgiveness. However, this is certainly not the case for anyone who is seeking God's forgiveness.

How can I forgive someone who has hurt me deeply?

MATTHEW 6:14-15 | *If you forgive those who sin against you, your heavenly Father will forgive you. But if you refuse to forgive others, your Father will not forgive your sins.*

Being unwilling to forgive shows that you have not understood or benefited from God's forgiveness.

MATTHEW 5:44 | *Love your enemies! Pray for those who persecute you!*

Pray for those who hate and hurt you. This releases you from the destructive emotions of anger, bitterness, and revenge and helps you to forgive those who have hurt you.

LUKE 23:34 | *Jesus said, "Father, forgive them, for they don't know what they are doing."*

Be more concerned about your offenders and less about nursing your own grudges and self-pity.

1 PETER 3:9 | *Don't repay evil for evil. Don't retaliate with insults when people insult you. Instead, pay them back with a blessing. That is what God has called you to do, and he will bless you for it.*

When people say hurtful things about you, God wants you to respond by blessing them.

EPHESIANS 4:31 | *Get rid of all bitterness, rage, anger, harsh words, and slander, as well as all types of evil behavior.*

An unforgiving attitude not only ruins your relationships but also poisons your soul. The person most hurt by unforgiveness is you.

Promise from God ISAIAH 43:25 | *I—yes, I alone—will blot out your sins for my own sake and will never think of them again.*

FRIENDSHIP

What does true friendship look like?

1 SAMUEL 18:1, 3-4 | *After David had finished talking with Saul, he met Jonathan, the king's son. There was an immediate bond between them. . . . Jonathan made a solemn pact with David, because he loved him as he loved himself. Jonathan sealed the pact by taking off his robe and giving it to David, together with his tunic, sword, bow, and belt.*

PROVERBS 17:17 | *A friend is always loyal, and a brother is born to help in time of need.*

Some friendships are fleeting and some are lasting. True friendships are glued together with bonds of loyalty and commitment. They remain intact, despite changing external circumstances.

What gets in the way of friendships?

1 SAMUEL 18:8-11 | *Saul [was] very angry. "What's this?" he said. "They credit David with ten thousands and me with only thousands. Next they'll be making him their king!" So from that time on Saul kept a jealous eye on David. The very next day . . . David was playing the harp. . . . Saul had a spear in*

his hand, and he suddenly hurled it at David, intending to pin him to the wall.

Jealousy is the great dividing force of friendships. Envy over what a friend has will soon turn to anger and bitterness, causing you to separate yourself from the one you truly cared for.

PSALM 41:9 | *Even my best friend, the one I trusted completely, . . . has turned against me.*

When respect and trust are seriously damaged, even the closest friendship is at risk.

Promise from God LEVITICUS 26:12 | *I will walk among you; I will be your God.*

FRUSTRATION

See also **PATIENCE**

How should I respond to frustration?

GENESIS 3:17-19 | *The ground is cursed because of you. All your life you will struggle to scratch a living from it. It will grow thorns and thistles for you, though you will eat of its grains. By the sweat of your brow will you have food to eat.*

While you don't welcome frustration, you shouldn't be surprised by it. You live in a world with people who are out for themselves; therefore you can expect obstacles and resistance in all forms. When you realize and accept frustration as a part of everyday life, you are better prepared to handle it in a positive way.

PROVERBS 21:2 | *People may be right in their own eyes, but the LORD examines their heart.*

Examining the source of your frustration helps you know how to deal with it. There is a big difference between being frustrated in your quest to do good and being frustrated because you are not getting your way. Each frustration must be dealt with individually.

EXODUS 17:4 | *Moses cried out to the LORD, "What should I do with these people?"*

JOHN 6:7 | *Philip [said], "Even if we worked for months, we wouldn't have enough money to feed them!"*

Recognize that many of your problems don't have a human solution. You must take them to God.

JOSHUA 1:9 | *Be strong and courageous! Do not be afraid or discouraged. For the LORD your God is with you wherever you go.*

Don't be discouraged. God will give you strength and courage to see you through.

Promise from God 1 CHRONICLES 28:20 | *Be strong and courageous, and do the work. Don't be afraid or discouraged, for the LORD God, my God, is with you. . . . He will see to it that all the work . . . is finished correctly.*

GOALS

See also **ACCOMPLISHMENTS, OPPORTUNITIES, SUCCESS**

Why are goals important?

MARK 10:45 | *Even the Son of Man came not to be served but to serve others and to give his life as a ransom for many.*

Goals keep you focused on your primary mission. No matter what was going on around him, Jesus never lost sight of the reason he came to earth.

JOB 6:11 | *I don't have the strength to endure. I have nothing to live for.*

Goals give you strength and endurance and purpose.

PSALM 40:8 | *I take joy in doing your will, my God, for your instructions are written on my heart.*

Good goals bring joy.

PROVERBS 4:25-27 | *Look straight ahead, and fix your eyes on what lies before you. Mark out a straight path for your feet; stay on the safe path. Don't get sidetracked; keep your feet from following evil.*

Goals help you keep your eyes on what you are pursuing.

Promise from God PSALM 37:4 | *Take delight in the LORD, and he will give you your heart's desires.*

GRIEF

See also **BROKEN HEART, COMFORT**

What might cause me to grieve?

RUTH 1:9 | *She kissed them good-bye, and they all broke down and wept.*

You grieve when you have to say good-bye to people you love.

NEHEMIAH 2:2-3 | *The king asked me, "Why are you looking so sad?" . . . I replied, ". . . The city where my ancestors are buried is in ruins, and the gates have been destroyed by fire."*

You grieve when you see loved ones hurt or in great need.

JOHN 11:13, 35 | *Lazarus had died. . . . Then Jesus wept.*

ACTS 9:37, 39 | *She became ill and died. . . . The room was filled with widows who were weeping.*

You grieve over the death of a loved one.

How do I get over my grief?

GENESIS 50:1 | *Joseph threw himself on his father and wept over him.*

2 SAMUEL 18:33 | *The king was overcome with emotion. He went up to the room over the gateway and burst into tears. And as he went, he cried, "O my son Absalom! My son, my son Absalom!"*

Recognize that grieving is necessary and important. You need the freedom to grieve. It is an important part of healing because it allows you to release the emotional pressure of your sorrow.

GENESIS 23:1-4 | *When Sarah was 127 years old, she died. . . . Abraham mourned and wept for her. Then, leaving her body, he said to the Hittite elders, ". . . Please sell me a piece of land so I can give my wife a proper burial."*

Take time to personally mourn, but also become involved in the steps necessary to bring closure to your loss. You grieve because you have lost something that was important to you.

Being involved in the process of grieving is a way of honoring what was meaningful.

ECCLESIASTES 3:1, 4 | *For everything there is a season. . . . A time to cry and a time to laugh. A time to grieve and a time to dance.*

Grief has its season, and its season may last a long while. But eventually God wants you to move on and comfort others who grieve. When that time comes, you need to let go of your grief or risk being stuck there and unable to properly function.

ISAIAH 66:12-13 | *The LORD says: . . . "I will comfort you . . . as a mother comforts her child."*

2 CORINTHIANS 1:3 | *God is our merciful Father and the source of all comfort.*

God knows you grieve, understands your sorrow, and comforts you. He does not promise to totally eliminate grief from your life, but he does promise to help you through it.

How can I help others who are grieving?

PSALM 69:20 | *If only one person would show some pity; if only one would turn and comfort me.*

PROVERBS 25:20 | *Singing cheerful songs to a person with a heavy heart is like taking someone's coat in cold weather or pouring vinegar in a wound.*

ROMANS 12:15 | *Weep with those who weep.*

Give your attention, sympathy, and comfort to the grieving. Pretending that the pain is not there is like rubbing salt in a wound. It is difficult to be with someone who is grieving, but you don't need to come up with the right words to make it all go away. You can't. Your concern and presence will help a grieving person more than words.

PROVERBS 15:13 | *A glad heart makes a happy face; a broken heart crushes the spirit.*

PROVERBS 17:22 | *A cheerful heart is good medicine, but a broken spirit saps a person's strength.*

Be aware of the toll that being brokenhearted takes on a person's spirit, mind, and body. Awareness leads to sympathy, sympathy leads to soothing the wounded, and soothing the wounded leads to healing.

2 CORINTHIANS 1:4 | *He comforts us in all our troubles so that we can comfort others. When they are troubled, we will be able to give them the same comfort God has given us.*

Share your experiences of God's comfort. Others may begin the healing process because of you.

1 PETER 5:12 | *I have written and sent this short letter to you . . . to encourage you.*

Encourage the brokenhearted.

JOB 16:2 | *I have heard all this before. What miserable comforters you are!*

JOB 21:34 | *How can your empty clichés comfort me?*

Be careful with the words you use to those who are grieving. Explanations and clichés are rarely comforting. Love, sympathy, and the power of your presence are urgently needed. Sometimes the best comfort you can give is to just be there.

JOB 42:11 | *Then all his brothers, sisters, and former friends came and feasted with him in his home. And they consoled him and comforted him because of all the trials. . . . And each of them brought him a gift.*

MARK 16:10 | *[Mary] went to the disciples, who were grieving and weeping, and told them what had happened.*

You can support one another as family and friends.

Promise from God PSALM 147:3 | *[The LORD] heals the brokenhearted and bandages their wounds.*

HABITS

See also **PERSONAL DISCIPLINE, SELF-CONTROL**

What are some common bad habits?

1 JOHN 3:8 | *When people keep on sinning, it shows that they belong to the devil, who has been sinning since the beginning.*

Sinning is a habit none of us can completely break, but a pattern of sinful living with no adjustment in behavior shows that a person is not serious about making a change.

EXODUS 8:28, 32 | *"All right, go ahead," Pharaoh replied. "I will let you go." . . . But Pharaoh again became stubborn and refused to let the people go.*

Pharaoh developed a bad habit of lying to get what he wanted.

NUMBERS 11:1 | *The people began to complain about their hardship.*

During their wilderness journey, the Israelites developed a bad habit of complaining. Chronic complaining can quickly turn into bitterness.

PROVERBS 10:26 | *Lazy people irritate their employers, like vinegar to the teeth or smoke in the eyes.*

Having too much time and too little to do can be fertile ground for bad habits.

How can God help me deal with bad habits?

ROMANS 7:15, 25 | *[Paul said,] "I don't really understand myself, for I want to do what is right, but I don't do it. Instead, I do what I hate. . . . The answer is in Jesus Christ."*

The apostle Paul knew that he could not kick the habit of sin completely. But he also knew that, with God's help, he could make progress every day. In the same way, a person may have to give up a habit in phases, one step at a time.

ROMANS 6:12-14 | *Do not let sin control the way you live; do not give in to sinful desires. Do not let any part of your body become an instrument . . . to serve sin. Instead, give yourselves completely to God. . . . Use your whole body as an instrument to do what is right for the glory of God. Sin is no longer your master. . . . [Now] you live under the freedom of God's grace.*

One of Satan's great lies is that you are a victim, with no power to resist some of the powerful influences around you. The world teaches you that heredity, environment, and circumstances excuse you from responsibility. But God is more powerful than anything that seeks to control you.

1 JOHN 2:15 | *Do not love this world nor the things it offers you, for when you love the world, you do not have the love of the Father in you.*

Indulging in bad habits often feels good even though a person knows they are ultimately bad. Breaking a bad habit can be hard because a person is losing something he or she enjoys. Understand that there may be a grieving process, but losing a bad habit ultimately brings a deeper satisfaction.

COLOSSIANS 3:2 | *Think about the things of heaven, not the things of earth.*

It will be much easier to break bad habits if one replaces them with good habits, which a person can learn from studying Jesus' life.

What are some good habits God can help me cultivate?

GENESIS 26:21-22 | *Isaac's men then dug another well, but again there was a dispute over it. . . . Abandoning that one, Isaac moved on and dug another well. This time there was no dispute over it.*

Isaac pursued a habit of living in peace. In this case, it meant staying away from the source of the conflict, the Philistines, even at great personal cost.

PSALM 28:7 | *The LORD is my strength and shield. I trust him with all my heart. He helps me, and my heart is filled with joy. I burst out in songs of thanksgiving.*

As a young boy, David developed the habits of talking to God, singing songs about him, and writing psalms. These helped him to trust in and follow God all his life.

Promise from God ROMANS 8:6 | *Letting your sinful nature control your mind leads to death. But letting the Spirit control your mind leads to life and peace.*

HELP

In what ways does God help me?

2 CHRONICLES 15:4 | *Whenever they were in trouble and turned to the LORD, the God of Israel, and sought him out, they found him.*

God helps you by always being available—he is present to help you whenever you call out to him. Prayer is the lifeline that connects you to God for daily help.

PHILIPPIANS 4:19 | *God . . . will supply all your needs from his glorious riches, which have been given to us in Christ Jesus.*

JAMES 1:5 | *If you need wisdom, ask our generous God, and he will give it to you. He will not rebuke you for asking.*

God helps you by providing resources to meet your needs. God has a full supply house and a ready supply system. It's free for the taking, but you must ask.

DEUTERONOMY 33:29 | *[The Lord] is your protecting shield and your triumphant sword!*

PSALM 28:7 | *The LORD is my strength and shield. I trust him with all my heart. He helps me, and my heart is filled with joy.*

God helps you by giving you strength to face any crisis.

ISAIAH 30:21 | *Right behind you a voice will say, "This is the way you should go," whether to the right or to the left.*

God helps you through his Holy Spirit, giving you an extra measure of wisdom, discernment, and guidance.

ROMANS 8:26 | *The Holy Spirit helps us in our weakness. For example, we don't know what God wants us to pray for. But the Holy Spirit prays for us with groanings that cannot be expressed in words.*

God, through his Holy Spirit, helps you to pray, even when you don't know how to pray or what to say.

GENESIS 2:18 | *The LORD God said, "It is not good for the man to be alone. I will make a helper who is just right for him."*

God helps you by sending you other people to love and support you.

How can I help others?

1 JOHN 3:17 | *If someone has enough money to live well and sees a brother or sister in need but shows no compassion—how can God's love be in that person?*

You can help others by sharing your abundance with those who have less. Be open to opportunities that come to you.

ISAIAH 1:17 | *Learn to do good. Seek justice. Help the oppressed. Defend the cause of orphans. Fight for the rights of widows.*

God works through willing people to provide his divine help. The poor, orphans, and widows are some of many who may need your help.

ECCLESIASTES 4:9-10 | *Two people are better off than one, for they can help each other succeed. If one person falls, the other can reach out and help. But someone who falls alone is in real trouble.*

You can help others by being available. When people try to do things all by themselves, they are limited by their weaknesses. But when they reach out for help, you can compensate for their weaknesses with your strengths.

Promise from God HEBREWS 13:6 | *We can say with confidence, "The LORD is my helper."*

HONESTY

See also **CONSCIENCE, INTEGRITY, TRUTH**

Why is it so important to be honest?

MATTHEW 12:33 | *A tree is identified by its fruit. If a tree is good, its fruit will be good.*

LUKE 16:10 | *If you are dishonest in little things, you won't be honest with greater responsibilities.*

Your level of honesty demonstrates the quality of your character.

1 TIMOTHY 1:19 | *Keep your conscience clear. For some people have deliberately violated their consciences; as a result, their faith has been shipwrecked.*

Honesty brings a clear conscience.

DEUTERONOMY 25:13-15 | *You must use accurate scales when you weigh out merchandise, and you must use full and honest measures . . . so that you may enjoy a long life.*

Dishonesty and deception hide selfish motives. Honesty brings freedom from guilt and from the consequences of deceptive actions.

2 KINGS 22:7 | *Don't require the construction supervisors to keep account of the money they receive, for they are honest and trustworthy men.*

Striving for honesty helps you develop a reputation of integrity. Consistent honesty in the past and present builds trust for continued honesty in the future.

ISAIAH 33:15-16 | *Those who are honest and fair, who refuse to profit by fraud, who stay far away from bribes, . . . who shut their eyes to all enticement to do wrong—these are the ones who will dwell on high.*

Striving for honesty will help you experience the benefits of God's ultimate justice and protection.

PSALM 37:37 | *Look at those who are honest and good, for a wonderful future awaits those who love peace.*

Striving for honesty helps you to enjoy life because you can live at peace with God and yourself.

Does honesty always mean telling everything I know?

PROVERBS 29:20 | *There is more hope for a fool than for someone who speaks without thinking.*

ECCLESIASTES 3:1, 7 | *For everything there is a season, a time for every activity under heaven. . . . A time to be quiet and a time to speak.*

COLOSSIANS 4:6 | *Let your conversation be gracious and attractive so that you will have the right response for everyone.*

Honesty should not be confused with gossip. Just because you know something doesn't mean you have to tell everyone about it. Honesty also involves integrity, making sure that what you say is helpful and builds others up rather than tears them down. The person who thinks before speaking is the wisest. It is not deceitful to withhold information that others don't need to know unless, of course, you are under oath in a court of law.

Promise from God PROVERBS 12:19 | *Truthful words stand the test of time, but lies are soon exposed.*

HONOR

See also **DUTY, INTEGRITY**

What is honor?

ECCLESIASTES 9:10 | *Whatever you do, do well.*

Honor is a recognition of outstanding contributions. It's a distinction of esteem that is earned. How you do what you do reveals what you believe and are committed to. Hard work done with excellence and integrity honors God, the people you serve under, your family, and yourself. Pursuing excellence is a hallmark of honor.

Why does honor matter?

EZEKIEL 18:5-9 | *Suppose a certain man is righteous and does what is just and right. . . . He does not commit adultery. . . . He is a merciful creditor . . . [and] does not rob the poor but instead gives food to the hungry and provides clothes for the needy. He grants loans without interest, stays away from injustice, is honest and fair when judging others, and faithfully obeys my decrees and regulations. Anyone who does these things is just and will surely live, says the Sovereign LORD.*

ROMANS 12:17 | *Do things in such a way that everyone can see you are honorable.*

It is often argued that one's personal life does not really matter so long as he or she performs the job well. God, however, does not make a distinction between our public and private lives. Justice, righteousness, integrity, mercy, honesty, and fairness are core traits of an honorable character because they reflect who a person really is. They also demonstrate what is truly important in life—loving, honoring, and respecting God and others.

1 THESSALONIANS 5:11-13 | *Encourage each other and build each other up, just as you are already doing. Dear brothers and sisters, honor those who are your leaders. . . . Show them great respect and wholehearted love because of their work.*

Honor never treats people as if they were invisible; it acknowledges the accomplishments and authority that they have earned and should be respected for. Honor is an attitude of thankfulness for what a person has done on behalf of others. When you honor a person, you are saying, "I value you."

Who deserves honor?

ROMANS 13:7 | *Give respect and honor to those who are in authority.*

Your superiors deserve honor—the people who train you and whom you interact with on a regular basis as well as the top leaders you may never see. Their experience will guide and develop your skills so you can have the most impact.

EXODUS 20:12 | *Honor your father and mother. Then you will live a long, full life in the land the LORD your God is giving you.*

The way you live honors your parents and what they taught you. As an adult, it's also important to think of ways that you can give back to them.

ROMANS 12:10 | *Love each other with genuine affection, and take delight in honoring each other.*

Every member of your team deserves your esteem; be sure to let them know that they are valued.

1 TIMOTHY 5:1 | *Never speak harshly to an older man, but appeal to him respectfully as you would to your own father.*

People who have sacrificed and paved the way for the younger generation should be honored for what they have done.

How is honor demonstrated?

ROMANS 13:3 | *Would you like to live without fear of the authorities? Do what is right, and they will honor you.*

By obeying authorities, both as a service member and as a civilian.

2 SAMUEL 9:7 | *"Don't be afraid!" David said. "I intend to show kindness to you because of my promise to your father, Jonathan."*

Honor is exemplified by acts of compassion. David's compassion to Jonathan's son showed his gracious heart, generosity, and integrity.

ROMANS 13:7 | *Give to everyone what you owe them: Pay your taxes and government fees to those who collect them.*

Paying your debts in a timely manner is honoring your commitments. This isn't saying you can never have a home mortgage or car payments, but it does mean that when payments are due, you must pay them promptly, honoring your commitments.

JOHN 5:19 | *Jesus explained, "I tell you the truth, the Son can do nothing by himself. He does only what he sees the Father doing."*

If you, like Jesus, continually seek what God would have you do, then you are more likely to make good choices that are honorable.

NUMBERS 30:2 | *A man who makes a vow to the LORD or makes a pledge under oath must never break it.*

You honor others by keeping your promises. Do not make promises quickly, and do not take them lightly.

Promise from God PROVERBS 3:35 | *The wise inherit honor, but fools are put to shame!*

HOPE

Where does hope come from?

PSALM 71:5 | *O Lord, you alone are my hope. I've trusted you, O LORD, from childhood.*

The Lord himself is the source of hope because his character is unchanging, his love is steadfast, his promises will all come true, and his omnipotence determines our future.

How can I keep hoping when God never seems to act?

ROMANS 8:24-25 | *If we already have something, we don't need to hope for it. But if we look forward to something we don't yet have, we must wait patiently and confidently.*

Hope, by definition, is expecting something that has not yet occurred. Once hope is fulfilled, it isn't hope anymore. Thus the practical outworking of hope is patience.

HEBREWS 11:1 | *Faith is the confidence that what we hope for will actually happen; it gives us assurance about things we cannot see.*

Have faith in God to do what he has promised, and trust that he will. Your hopes are not idle hopes but are built on the solid foundation of his trustworthiness.

JEREMIAH 29:11 | *"I know the plans I have for you," says the LORD. "They are plans for good and not for disaster, to give you a future and a hope."*

Where can I go to strengthen my hope?

ROMANS 15:4 | *Such things were written in the Scriptures long ago to teach us. And the Scriptures give us hope and encouragement as we wait patiently for God's promises.*

PSALM 119:81, 114 | *I am worn out waiting for your rescue, but I have put my hope in your word. . . . You are my refuge and my shield; your word is my source of hope.*

Each day you can visit God's Word and have your hope renewed and reinforced. His Word never fails or wavers.

What can I do when things seem hopeless?

1 SAMUEL 1:10 | *Hannah was in deep anguish, crying bitterly as she prayed to the LORD.*

You can pray. In the midst of Hannah's hopelessness, she prayed to God, knowing that if any hope were to be found, it would be found in him.

PSALM 27:14 | *Wait patiently for the LORD. Be brave and courageous.*

You can remember that God's timing is perfect.

PSALM 18:4-6 | *The ropes of death entangled me; floods of destruction swept over me. The grave wrapped its ropes around me; death laid a trap in my path. But in my distress I cried out to the LORD; yes, I prayed to my God for help. He heard me from his sanctuary; my cry to him reached his ears.*

You can remember that sin and evil may sometimes thwart your plans here on earth but cannot affect God's plans in heaven.

Promise from God   PSALM 130:7   I *Hope in the LORD; for with the LORD there is unfailing love. His redemption overflows.*

HUMILITY

See also **PRIDE**

What is true humility?

ZEPHANIAH 3:12   I   *Those who are left will be the lowly and humble, for it is they who trust in the name of the LORD.*

Humility is not thinking too highly of yourself.

MATTHEW 18:4   I   *Anyone who becomes as humble as this little child is the greatest in the Kingdom of Heaven.*

Humility is childlike. It is an attitude of total trust in a great God.

TITUS 3:2   I   *[Believers] must not slander anyone and must avoid quarreling. Instead, they should be gentle and show true humility to everyone.*

Humility is truly caring about others and looking out for their best interests.

PSALM 51:3-4   I   *I recognize my rebellion; it haunts me day and night. Against you, and you alone, have I sinned; I have done what is evil in your sight. You will be proved right in what you say, and your judgment against me is just.*

Humility is willingness to admit and confess sin.

PROVERBS 12:23 | *The wise don't make a show of their knowledge, but fools broadcast their foolishness.*

Humility is refraining from proving what you know, how good you are at something, or that you are always right.

PROVERBS 13:10 | *Pride leads to conflict; those who take advice are wise.*

Humility allows you to ask for advice.

GENESIS 32:9-10 | *Jacob prayed, "O God . . . you promised me, 'I will treat you kindly.' I am not worthy of all the unfailing love and faithfulness you have shown to me, your servant."*

Humility comes when you recognize your need for God and then acknowledge how he provides for you.

How do I become humble?

DEUTERONOMY 8:2-3 | *[Moses said to the people of Israel,] "Remember how the LORD your God led you through the wilderness for these forty years, humbling you and testing you to prove your character, and to find out whether or not you would obey his commands. Yes, he humbled you by letting you go hungry and then feeding you with manna. . . . He did it to teach you that people do not live by bread alone."*

Humility comes when you recognize that you need God.

1 PETER 3:8 | *All of you should be of one mind. Sympathize with each other. Love each other as brothers and sisters. Be tenderhearted, and keep a humble attitude.*

Humility comes from developing a sympathetic and tender heart toward others.

PHILIPPIANS 2:3 | *Don't be selfish; don't try to impress others. Be humble, thinking of others as better than yourselves.*

Humility means thinking of others' welfare before thinking about your own.

1 PETER 5:5 | *You younger men must accept the authority of the elders. And all of you, serve each other in humility, for "God opposes the proud but favors the humble."*

Serving other people will develop humility in you. Humility also means accepting the authority of those over you.

Promise from God ISAIAH 57:15 | *The high and lofty one who lives in eternity, the Holy One, says this: "I live in the high and holy place with those whose spirits are contrite and humble. I restore the crushed spirit of the humble and revive the courage of those with repentant hearts."*

INTEGRITY

See also **CHARACTER, HONESTY, HONOR**

What is integrity?

PSALM 15:1-2 | *Who may worship in your sanctuary, LORD? Who may enter your presence on your holy hill? Those who lead blameless lives and do what is right, speaking the truth from sincere hearts.*

Integrity means living a life that is consistent in belief and behavior, in words and deeds.

PROVERBS 11:5 | *The godly are directed by honesty; the wicked fall beneath their load of sin.*

Integrity should be your guiding principle of life and relationships.

PROVERBS 16:11 | *The LORD demands accurate scales and balances; he sets the standards for fairness.*

LUKE 16:10 | *If you are faithful in little things, you will be faithful in large ones. But if you are dishonest in little things, you won't be honest with greater responsibilities.*

2 CORINTHIANS 4:2 | *We reject all shameful deeds and underhanded methods. We don't try to trick anyone or distort the word of God. We tell the truth before God, and all who are honest know this.*

Integrity is measured in small decisions and choices made when no one else is watching. Every choice a person makes will one day come to light.

What is the importance of integrity?

PROVERBS 10:9 | *People with integrity walk safely, but those who follow crooked paths will slip and fall.*

PROVERBS 12:3 | *Wickedness never brings stability, but the godly have deep roots.*

Integrity provides stability. Each step away from a life of integrity is a step closer to a "slippery slope" that leads into a compromised lifestyle.

PSALM 25:21 | *May integrity and honesty protect me, for I put my hope in you.*

PROVERBS 11:3 | *Honesty guides good people; dishonesty destroys treacherous people.*

Integrity provides protection and guidance. Lack of integrity exposes you to all kinds of harm, especially the disintegration of your own character.

How can I develop integrity in my life?

PROVERBS 2:1-2, 5, 9 | *My child, listen to what I say, and treasure my commands. Tune your ears to wisdom, and concentrate on understanding. . . . Then you will understand what it means to fear the LORD, and you will gain knowledge of God. . . . Then you will understand what is right, just, and fair, and you will find the right way to go.*

Cultivating a right relationship with God and living a life based on God's Word are two essential means to a life of integrity. Look to God's Word, for therein is the standard of integrity.

How do I demonstrate integrity?

DANIEL 6:4 | *The other administrators and high officers began searching for some fault in the way Daniel was handling government affairs, but they couldn't find anything to criticize or condemn. He was faithful, always responsible, and completely trustworthy.*

TITUS 2:7-8 | *You yourself must be an example to them by doing good works of every kind. Let everything you do reflect the integrity and seriousness of your teaching. Teach the truth so that your teaching can't be criticized. Then those who oppose us will be ashamed and have nothing bad to say about us.*

You demonstrate integrity by the way you conduct yourself and the way you treat others. Your words and actions are to be consistent and above reproach.

JOB 27:4-6 | *My lips will speak no evil, and my tongue will speak no lies. . . . I will defend my integrity until I die. I will maintain my innocence without wavering. My conscience is clear for as long as I live.*

1 TIMOTHY 1:19 | *Cling to your faith in Christ, and keep your conscience clear. For some people have deliberately violated their consciences; as a result, their faith has been shipwrecked.*

You demonstrate integrity by keeping your conscience clear before God and others.

DEUTERONOMY 16:19 | *You must never twist justice or show partiality. Never accept a bribe, for bribes blind the eyes of the wise and corrupt the decisions of the godly.*

You demonstrate integrity by refusing to twist justice, show partiality, or take bribes.

ROMANS 12:21 | *Don't let evil conquer you, but conquer evil by doing good.*

1 PETER 2:12 | *Be careful to live properly among your unbelieving neighbors. Then even if they accuse you of doing wrong, they will see your honorable behavior, and they will give honor to God when he judges the world.*

You demonstrate your integrity when you guard your every move and seek support and accountability to ensure that you maintain integrity in the face of every test.

Promise from God MICAH 6:8 | *O people, the LORD has told you what is good, and this is what he requires of you: to do what is right, to love mercy, and to walk humbly with your God.*

JUDGING OTHERS

See also **PREJUDICE**

Why is it wrong to judge others?

1 CORINTHIANS 4:5 | *Don't make judgments about anyone ahead of time—before the Lord returns. For he will bring our darkest secrets to light and will reveal our private motives. Then God will give to each one whatever praise is due.*

Be very slow to judge others, because only God is capable of judging perfectly every time.

ROMANS 2:1 | *You may think you can condemn such people, but you are just as bad, and you have no excuse! When you say they are wicked and should be punished, you are condemning yourself, for you who judge others do these very same things.*

When you condemn others for their sin without first carefully considering your own sin, God sees your hypocrisy.

1 SAMUEL 16:7 | *The LORD said to Samuel, "Don't judge by his appearance or height, for I have rejected him. The LORD doesn't see things the way you see them. People judge by outward appearance, but the LORD looks at the heart."*

God doesn't want you to make judgments based on what you see.

LEVITICUS 19:15 | *Do not twist justice in legal matters by favoring the poor or being partial to the rich and powerful. Always judge people fairly.*

When you have to make a judgment, do so with fairness and integrity.

What are the consequences of judging others?

2 SAMUEL 12:5-7 | *David was furious. "As surely as the LORD lives," he vowed, "any man who would do such a thing deserves to die! He must repay four lambs to the poor man for the one he stole and for having no pity." Then Nathan said to David, "You are that man!"*

If you are too quick to judge others, you may be found guilty of the same things.

MATTHEW 7:2 | *You will be treated as you treat others. The standard you use in judging is the standard by which you will be judged.*

LUKE 6:37 | *Do not condemn others, or it will all come back against you. Forgive others, and you will be forgiven.*

You will be judged by the same standard you use, so it's better to be merciful and forgiving than harsh and critical.

Promise from God MATTHEW 7:1 | *Do not judge others, and you will not be judged.*

JUSTICE

How can I work effectively for justice?

AMOS 5:21, 24 | *[The Lord says,] "I hate all your show and pretense—the hypocrisy of your religious festivals and solemn assemblies. . . . Instead, I want to see a mighty flood of justice, an endless river of righteous living."*

Make justice a top priority.

PSALM 82:3 | *Give justice to the poor and the orphan; uphold the rights of the oppressed and the destitute.*

Speak out against injustice.

ISAIAH 1:17 | *Learn to do good. Seek justice. Help the oppressed. Defend the cause of orphans. Fight for the rights of widows.*

Strive for justice with energy and dedication.

PSALM 106:3 | *There is joy for those who deal justly with others and always do what is right.*

ISAIAH 56:1 | *The LORD says: "Be just and fair to all. Do what is right and good, for I am coming soon to rescue you and to display my righteousness among you."*

ROMANS 13:7 | *Give to everyone what you owe them.*

Persist in doing what is right. Don't become unjust yourself.

PROVERBS 20:22 | *Don't say, "I will get even for this wrong." Wait for the LORD to handle the matter.*

Don't repay evil with evil. Work for justice without a vengeful spirit.

How do God's justice and mercy relate?

MATTHEW 5:43-44 | *[Jesus said,] "You have heard the law that says, 'Love your neighbor' and hate your enemy. But I say, love your enemies!"*

Justice punishes evil, crime, and wrongdoing. Mercy forgives the sinner. Jesus has set a new standard for mercy.

One of the hardest things you can do is forgive someone who has wronged you, but it is only through forgiveness that you can be free of the bitterness of injustice. Your mercy may be exactly what someone needs to understand God's mercy.

Promise from God   PSALM 58:11 | *Then at last everyone will say, "There truly is a reward for those who live for God; surely there is a God who judges justly here on earth."*

LEADERSHIP

See also **DELEGATION**

What are the qualities of a good leader?

DEUTERONOMY 1:12-13 | *[Moses said,] "How can I deal with all your problems and bickering? Choose some well-respected men from each tribe who are known for their wisdom and understanding, and I will appoint them as your leaders."*

A wise leader delegates some of his responsibilities to trustworthy subordinates.

MICAH 3:1 | *Listen, you leaders of Israel! You are supposed to know right from wrong.*

Good leaders are dedicated to doing what is right.

NEHEMIAH 5:9 | *I pressed further, "What you are doing is not right!"*

A good leader courageously confronts those who are doing what is wrong.

How can I know if and when I should exercise leadership?

DEUTERONOMY 3:28 | *Commission Joshua and encourage and strengthen him, for he will lead the people across the Jordan. He will give them all the land you now see before you as their possession.*

If you have been commissioned to lead, then lead!

Promise from God JEREMIAH 3:15 | *[The LORD says,] "I will give you shepherds after my own heart, who will guide you with knowledge and understanding."*

LISTENING

Why is listening so important?

PROVERBS 1:9 | *What you learn from [your father and mother] will crown you with grace and be a chain of honor around your neck.*

Listening helps you grow and mature. Good listening fosters learning, which leads to knowledge and wisdom.

PROVERBS 5:13-14 | *Oh, why didn't I listen to my teachers? Why didn't I pay attention to my instructors? I have come to the brink of utter ruin, and now I must face public disgrace.*

Listening helps keep you from making mistakes.

PROVERBS 8:6 | *Listen to me! For I have important things to tell you.*

Listening keeps you from being closed minded. It gives you the opportunity to hear a variety of ideas from many different sources.

EXODUS 18:24 | *Moses listened to his father-in-law's advice and followed his suggestions.*

Listening shows that you respect others. It honors their words, and they feel affirmed because you've listened to them.

PROVERBS 21:13 | *Those who shut their ears to the cries of the poor will be ignored in their own time of need.*

Listening is more than hearing; it connects you with others. It helps you know when they are in need and the best way to help them.

What are some things I shouldn't listen to?

MATTHEW 6:13 | *Don't let us yield to temptation.*

Temptation.

LEVITICUS 19:16 | *Do not spread slanderous gossip among your people.*

Gossip.

EPHESIANS 5:4 | *Obscene stories, foolish talk, and coarse jokes—these are not for you.*

Insults and off-color stories.

PROVERBS 13:5 | *The godly hate lies.*

Lies.

PROVERBS 29:5 | *To flatter friends is to lay a trap for their feet.*

Flattery.

How can I better listen to God?

PSALM 4:3 | *You can be sure of this: . . . The LORD will answer when I call to him.*

PSALM 5:3 | *Each morning I bring my requests to you and wait expectantly.*

Through prayer. After you talk to God, stay and listen for a while.

PSALM 46:10 | *Be still, and know that I am God!*

Being quiet helps you better hear God's voice. Find times and places where there's nothing else to hear but God's voice.

LUKE 8:18 | *Pay attention to how you hear. To those who listen to my teaching, more understanding will be given. But for those who are not listening, even what they think they understand will be taken away from them.*

When you think you've heard something from God, pay attention to it. Don't miss an opportunity for a lesson from the Master Teacher.

Promise from God PROVERBS 1:23 | *Come and listen to my counsel. I'll share my heart with you and make you wise.*

LONELINESS

Why does God allow me to be lonely?

1 SAMUEL 20:41 | *David bowed three times to Jonathan. . . . Both of them were in tears as they embraced each other and said good-bye, especially David.*

ACTS 15:39 | *Their disagreement was so sharp that they separated. Barnabas took John Mark with him and sailed for Cyprus.*

1 THESSALONIANS 2:17 | *Dear brothers and sisters, after we were separated from you for a little while (though our hearts never left you), we tried very hard to come back because of our intense longing to see you again.*

You will often be separated from friends and family for various reasons. Sometimes you are lonely because you have hurt those you care about and they have left you. Sometimes your friends stop being your friends for reasons you don't understand. And sometimes you have to say good-bye when a friend moves away or when you're stationed far from those you love. God doesn't want you to be lonely, but in this life he allows people's actions to take their natural course. In each of these circumstances, he promises to help you learn from it, and he promises never to leave you, always supplying you with comfort and strength when you ask.

ROMANS 8:38-39 | *Nothing can ever separate us from God's love. . . . Not even the powers of hell can separate us from God's love. . . . Indeed, nothing in all creation will ever be able to separate us from the love of God that is revealed in Christ Jesus our Lord.*

God has promised he will always be there for you. Nothing can separate you from him. When your human relationships fail, take comfort from your friendship with God.

How can God help me with loneliness?

PSALM 139:17 | *How precious are your thoughts about me, O God. They cannot be numbered!*

Recognize that you are not unlovable or deficient just because you are lonely. You have value because God made you, loves you, and promises never to leave you.

EXODUS 5:21-22 | *The foremen said to [Moses and Aaron], "May the LORD judge and punish you for making us stink before Pharaoh and his officials. . . ." Then Moses went back to the LORD and protested, "Why have you brought all this trouble on your own people, Lord? Why did you send me?"*

1 KINGS 19:4 | *[Elijah] went on alone into the wilderness, traveling all day. He sat down under a solitary broom tree and prayed that he might die.*

Loneliness can cause you to feel sorry for yourself, become discouraged, and fall prey to temptation. Don't give up on God when you are lonely. Be careful not to separate yourself from the One who wants to be with you always.

ISAIAH 41:10 | *Don't be afraid, for I am with you. Don't be discouraged, for I am your God. I will strengthen you and help you. I will hold you up with my victorious right hand.*

Loneliness can cause fear. But knowing that God is with you and fighting for you can calm your fears.

How can I help those who are lonely?

JAMES 1:27 | *Pure and genuine religion in the sight of God the Father means caring for orphans and widows in their distress.*

3 JOHN 1:5 | *You are being faithful to God when you care for the traveling teachers who pass through, even though they are strangers to you.*

Befriend them. Often in caring for those who are lonely, your need for company will be met as well.

Promise from God HEBREWS 13:5 | *God has said, "I will never fail you. I will never abandon you."*

LOVE

What is love?

1 CORINTHIANS 13:4-7 | *Love is patient and kind. Love is not jealous or boastful or proud or rude. It does not demand its own way. It is not irritable, and it keeps no record of being wronged. It does not rejoice about injustice but rejoices whenever the truth wins out. Love never gives up, never loses faith, is always hopeful, and endures through every circumstance.*

These words are some of the most eloquent and accurate descriptions of love ever written. Love is a commitment and a choice of conduct that produces powerful feelings. If you practice the qualities and behaviors described in these verses, you will experience satisfaction and fulfillment beyond imagination.

MATTHEW 10:42 | *If you give even a cup of cold water to one of the least of my followers, you will surely be rewarded.*

Love looks for opportunities to help those in deep need.

JOHN 15:13 | *There is no greater love than to lay down one's life for one's friends.*

Love is willing to sacrifice for the good of others, even unto death.

Promise from God ROMANS 8:39 | *No power in the sky above or in the earth below—indeed, nothing in all creation will ever be able to separate us from the love of God that is revealed in Christ Jesus our Lord.*

LOYALTY

See also **COMMITMENT**

Why is loyalty important?

PROVERBS 3:3-4 | *Never let loyalty and kindness leave you! Tie them around your neck as a reminder. Write them deep within your heart. Then you will find favor with both God and people, and you will earn a good reputation.*

PROVERBS 19:22 | *Loyalty makes a person attractive. It is better to be poor than dishonest.*

Loyalty to others is essential for the integrity of relationships and their effectiveness. Without loyalty, others become a means to an end and are not valued for who they are as persons.

What are the benefits of loyalty?

RUTH 1:16 | *Wherever you go, I will go; wherever you live, I will live. Your people will be my people, and your God will be my God.*

You may find that loyalty is not only a way to value those God has brought into your life, but it also may open the doors to other benefits.

1 SAMUEL 19:6-7 | *Saul listened to Jonathan and vowed, "As surely as the LORD lives, David will not be killed." Afterward Jonathan . . . told [David] what had happened.*

Loyalty not only brings the satisfaction of integrity in a relationship but may also bring practical benefits such as protection and care for your welfare. Jonathan's loyalty to David was instrumental in saving David's life on more than one occasion.

ACTS 15:37-39 | *Barnabas agreed and wanted to take along John Mark. But Paul disagreed strongly, since John Mark had deserted them in Pamphylia and had not continued with them in their work. Their disagreement was so sharp that they separated. Barnabas took John Mark with him and sailed for Cyprus.*

Loyalty can keep a relationship alive so that you can help in restoring someone who has failed. Barnabas's persistent loyalty to John Mark made it possible for John Mark to have another opportunity to prove himself—and he did.

Promise from God   PSALM 31:23 | *The LORD protects those who are loyal to him.*

MOTIVES

Do my motives matter?

1 SAMUEL 16:7 | *The LORD said to Samuel, "Don't judge by his appearance or height. . . . The LORD doesn't see things the way you see them. People judge by outward appearance, but the LORD looks at the heart."*

God is more concerned about your motives than your appearance or outward actions, because your motives determine what is in your heart.

How can I have purer motives?

1 CORINTHIANS 4:4 | *My conscience is clear, but that doesn't prove I'm right. It is the Lord himself who will examine me and decide.*

Remember that God alone knows your heart. Ask him to reveal to you any area in which your motives are less than pure.

PSALM 19:14 | *May the words of my mouth and the meditation of my heart be pleasing to you, O LORD, my rock and my redeemer.*

Ask God to change the way you think by changing your heart.

1 CHRONICLES 28:9 | *Learn to know . . . God . . . intimately. Worship and serve him with your whole heart and a willing mind. For the LORD sees every heart and knows every plan and thought.*

Your attitude toward God is a good indicator of your motives toward others. If you are halfhearted in the way you approach your relationship with God, chances are your motives toward others may be more halfhearted and self-centered than they should be.

PSALM 26:2 | *Put me on trial, LORD, and cross-examine me. Test my motives and my heart.*

PROVERBS 17:3 | *Fire tests the purity of silver and gold, but the LORD tests the heart.*

Welcome any test of your motives. This gives you an opportunity to grow.

PROVERBS 21:2 | *People may be right in their own eyes, but the LORD examines their heart.*

Before you do something, remember that God is as interested in your motives as he is in your actions.

Promise from God EZEKIEL 36:26 | *[The Lord says,] "I will give you a new heart, and I will put a new spirit in you. I will take out your stony, stubborn heart and give you a tender, responsive heart."*

OPPORTUNITIES

See also **GOALS**

How can I prepare for opportunities that might come my way?

MATTHEW 9:37-38 | *[Jesus] said to his disciples, "The harvest is great, but the workers are few. So pray."*

MATTHEW 26:40-41 | *[Jesus said to Peter,] "Couldn't you watch with me even one hour? Keep watch and pray, so that you will not give in to temptation. For the spirit is willing, but the body is weak!"*

Be alert and prayerful so you can recognize and respond to opportunities that come along.

GENESIS 39:3-4, 6 | *The LORD was with Joseph, giving him success in everything he did. This pleased Potiphar, so he soon made*

Joseph his personal attendant. He put him in charge of his entire household and everything he owned. . . . With Joseph there, he didn't worry about a thing.

GENESIS 41:1, 14, 39-40 | *Later, . . . Pharaoh sent for Joseph . . . and he was quickly brought from the prison. . . . Then Pharaoh said to Joseph, "Since God has revealed the meaning of the dreams to you, clearly no one else is as intelligent or wise as you are. You will be in charge of my court, and all my people will take orders from you. Only I, sitting on my throne, will have a rank higher than yours."*

Responsibility will open doors of opportunity. How you handle each responsibility determines whether or not you will be trusted with more. Joseph was unjustly thrown into prison. He could have whined and complained, become bitter and done nothing. Instead, he seized every opportunity he could in his situation, quickly became trusted for his responsibility, and eventually rose to even greater prominence in Egypt.

How can I make the most of opportunities?

DEUTERONOMY 1:21, 30 | *Don't be afraid! Don't be discouraged! . . . The LORD your God is going ahead of you. He will fight for you, just as you saw him do in Egypt.*

Respond with courage and faith in God when opportunities arise.

PHILIPPIANS 1:14 | *Because of my imprisonment, most of the believers here have gained confidence and boldly speak God's message without fear.*

Seize opportunities that come along, even when you are experiencing personal hardship.

1 CORINTHIANS 16:8-9 | *I will be staying here at Ephesus until the Festival of Pentecost. There is a wide-open door for a great work here.*

Be flexible so you are able to change your plans in order to take advantage of an opportunity.

ACTS 21:37 | *As Paul was about to be taken inside, he said to the commander, "May I have a word with you?" "Do you know Greek?" the commander asked, surprised.*

Like Paul, use your intelligence to take advantage of an opportunity.

Promise from God MATTHEW 25:29 | *To those who use well what they are given, even more will be given, and they will have an abundance. But from those who do nothing, even what little they have will be taken away.*

PATIENCE

See also **FRUSTRATION**

Is patience really worth working for?

ROMANS 15:5 | *May God, who gives . . . patience and encouragement, help you live in complete harmony with each other, as is fitting for followers of Christ Jesus.*

GALATIANS 5:22-23 | *The Holy Spirit produces this kind of fruit in our lives: love, joy, peace, patience, kindness, goodness, faithfulness, gentleness, and self-control.*

COLOSSIANS 1:11 | *We also pray that you will be strengthened with all his glorious power so you will have all the endurance and patience you need. May you be filled with joy.*

Patience leads to harmony with others, endurance to handle difficult circumstances, and an expectant attitude of hope that things will get better.

HEBREWS 10:36 | *Patient endurance is what you need now, so that you will continue to do God's will. Then you will receive all that he has promised.*

Patience is evidence of strong character. As you pass each test of your patience, you will build a higher degree of patience for when you are tested again.

JAMES 5:7-8 | *Consider the farmers who patiently wait for the rains in the fall and in the spring. They eagerly look for the valuable harvest to ripen. You, too, must be patient.*

Whether you're waiting for crops to ripen or orders to come through, you can grow in patience by recognizing that these things take time and there is only so much you can do to help them along.

How do I develop more patience?

EXODUS 5:22; 6:2 | *Moses went back to the LORD and protested, . . . "Why did you send me?" . . . And God said to Moses, "I am Yahweh—'the LORD.'"*

Focusing less on your agenda and more on God's agenda for you will provide a "big picture" perspective and help you be less impatient.

HABAKKUK 2:3 | *If it seems slow in coming, wait patiently, for it will surely take place. It will not be delayed.*

Patience can actually give you an attitude of excited anticipation for each new day. If God is going to do what is best for you, then his plan for you will be accomplished on his schedule, not yours. Keeping that in mind, you can actually become excited about waiting for him to act, for you wake up each day anticipating what good thing he will work in your life that is just right for you at the present time.

2 TIMOTHY 2:24 | *A servant of the Lord must not quarrel but must be kind to everyone, be able to teach, and be patient with difficult people.*

God develops patience in you through your relationships with others. Abrasive relationships teach you to patiently endure. But even in loving relationships, patience is necessary.

1 PETER 2:19-20 | *God is pleased with you when you do what you know is right and patiently endure unfair treatment. Of course, you get no credit for being patient if you are beaten for doing wrong. But if you suffer for doing good and endure it patiently, God is pleased with you.*

God uses life's circumstances to develop your patience. You can't always choose the circumstances that come your way, but you can choose how you will respond to them.

Promise from God ISAIAH 30:18 | *The LORD must wait for you to come to him so he can show you his love and compassion. For the LORD is a faithful God. Blessed are those who wait for his help.*

PEACE

See also **WAR**

How can I make peace with others?

PSALM 34:14 | *Search for peace, and work to maintain it.*

MATTHEW 5:9 | *God blesses those who work for peace.*

Peace is not the absence of conflict; it's assurance in the midst of conflict. Peace comes from dealing with conflict appropriately.

EPHESIANS 4:3 | *Make every effort to keep yourselves united in the Spirit, binding yourselves together with peace.*

Unity comes from always seeking peace.

PSALM 37:37 | *Look at those who are honest and good, for a wonderful future awaits those who love peace.*

ROMANS 12:17-19 | *Never pay back evil with more evil. . . . Do all that you can to live in peace with everyone. Dear friends, never take revenge. Leave that to . . . God.*

If you harbor thoughts of revenge, you are not at peace with others. Bitterness and revenge can never bring peacefulness.

PROVERBS 12:20 | *Deceit fills hearts that are plotting evil; joy fills hearts that are planning peace!*

Seeking peace with others is one of the surest ways to release streams of joy into your heart.

Promise from God JOHN 14:27 | *[Jesus said,] "I am leaving you with a gift—peace of mind and heart. And the peace I give is a gift the world cannot give. So don't be troubled or afraid."*

PERSONAL DISCIPLINE

See also **ENDURANCE, HABITS**

Why is personal discipline necessary?

PROVERBS 23:23 | *Get the truth and never sell it; also get wisdom, discipline, and good judgment.*

Personal discipline, not innate talent or intellect, is often the deciding factor between success and failure.

1 KINGS 10:23; 11:1, 4 | *King Solomon became richer and wiser than any other king on earth. . . . Now King Solomon loved many foreign women. . . . In Solomon's old age, they turned his heart to worship other gods instead of being completely faithful to the LORD his God, as his father, David, had been.*

A person's discipline, or lack thereof, greatly affects others' welfare.

How do I cultivate personal discipline?

PHILIPPIANS 3:12-15 | *I press on to possess that perfection for which Christ Jesus first possessed me. No, dear brothers and sisters, I have not achieved it, but I focus on this one thing: Forgetting the past and looking forward to what lies ahead, I press on to reach the end of the race and receive the heavenly prize for which God, through Christ Jesus, is calling us. Let all who are spiritually mature agree on these things.*

Discipline begins with passion and is sustained by power.

1 CORINTHIANS 9:24-26 | *Don't you realize that in a race everyone runs, but only one person gets the prize? So run to win! All*

athletes are disciplined in their training. They do it to win a prize that will fade away, but we do it for an eternal prize. So I run with purpose in every step.

Discipline is the link between your desires and achieving those desires. Self-control not only helps you achieve your goals but also helps you stay on track with them. Many people have been ruined by letting up on discipline once they have achieved their goals.

1 TIMOTHY 4:7-8 | *Train yourself to be godly. "Physical training is good, but training for godliness is much better, promising benefits in this life and in the life to come."*

Discipline requires time, effort, hard work, and sometimes even suffering. But training will pay off in a combat situation.

Promise from God   PROVERBS 1:7 | *Fear of the LORD is the foundation of true knowledge, but fools despise wisdom and discipline.*

PLANNING

Why is it important to plan ahead?

PROVERBS 20:4 | *Those too lazy to plow in the right season will have no food at the harvest.*

LUKE 14:28 | *Don't begin until you count the cost. For who would begin construction of a building without first calculating the cost to see if there is enough money to finish it?*

Planning is a necessary part of successful living.

PROVERBS 13:16 | *Wise people think before they act.*

PROVERBS 22:3 | *A prudent person foresees danger and takes precautions. The simpleton goes blindly on and suffers the consequences.*

Planning prepares you for life. Those who neglect to plan are caught off guard by difficult circumstances, but those who plan ahead are equipped to face the difficulties of life with confidence. Planning ahead allows you to be productive even in difficult times.

Promise from God PROVERBS 19:21 | *You can make many plans, but the LORD's purpose will prevail.*

PRAYER

What is prayer?

2 CHRONICLES 7:14 | *[The Lord said,] "If my people who are called by my name will humble themselves and pray and seek my face and turn from their wicked ways, I will hear from heaven."*

PSALM 140:6 | *I said to the LORD, "You are my God!" Listen, O LORD, to my cries for mercy!*

Prayer is conversation with God. It is simply talking with God and listening to him, honestly telling him your thoughts and feelings, praising him, thanking him, confessing sin, and asking for his help and advice. The essence of prayer is humbly entering the very presence of almighty God.

PSALM 38:18 | *I confess my sins; I am deeply sorry for what I have done.*

1 JOHN 1:9 | *If we confess our sins to him, he is faithful and just to forgive us our sins and to cleanse us.*

Prayer often begins with a confession of the things you have done wrong. It is through confession that you demonstrate the humility necessary for open lines of communication with the almighty, holy God.

1 SAMUEL 14:36 | *The priest said, "Let's ask God first."*

2 SAMUEL 5:19 | *David asked the LORD, "Should I go out to fight the Philistines?"*

Prayer is asking God for guidance and waiting for his direction and leading.

MARK 1:35 | *Before daybreak the next morning, Jesus got up and went out to an isolated place to pray.*

Prayer is an expression of an intimate relationship with the heavenly Father, who makes his own love and resources available to you. Just as you enjoy being with people you love, you enjoy spending time with God the more you get to know him and understand just how much he loves you.

1 SAMUEL 3:10 | *The LORD came and called as before, "Samuel! Samuel!" And Samuel replied, "Speak, your servant is listening."*

Good conversation also includes listening, so make time for God to speak to you. When you listen to God, he will make his wisdom known to you.

PSALM 9:1-2 | *I will praise you, LORD, with all my heart; I will tell of all the marvelous things you have done. I will be filled with joy because of you. I will sing praises to your name, O Most High.*

Through prayer you praise your mighty God.

Is there a "right" way to pray?

1 SAMUEL 23:2 | *David asked the LORD, "Should I go . . . ?"*

NEHEMIAH 1:4 | *For days I mourned, fasted, and prayed to the God of heaven.*

PSALM 18:1 | *I love you, LORD; you are my strength.*

PSALM 32:5 | *Finally, I confessed all my sins to you and stopped trying to hide my guilt. I said to myself, "I will confess my rebellion to the LORD." And you forgave me! All my guilt is gone.*

EPHESIANS 6:18 | *Pray in the Spirit at all times and on every occasion. Stay alert and be persistent in your prayers for all believers everywhere.*

Effective prayer includes elements of adoration, fasting, confession, petition, and persistence.

MATTHEW 6:9-13 | *[Jesus said,] "Pray like this: Our Father in heaven, may your name be kept holy. May your Kingdom come soon. May your will be done on earth, as it is in heaven. Give us today the food we need, and forgive us our sins, as we have forgiven those who sin against us. And don't let us yield to temptation, but rescue us from the evil one."*

Jesus taught his disciples that prayer is an intimate relationship with the Father that includes a dependency for daily needs, a commitment to obedience, and forgiveness of sin.

NEHEMIAH 2:4-5 | *The king asked, "Well, how can I help you?" With a [quick] prayer to the God of heaven, I replied.*

Prayer can be spontaneous.

Does God always answer prayer?

PSALM 116:1-2 | *I love the LORD because he hears my voice and my prayer for mercy. Because he bends down to listen, I will pray as long as I have breath!*

1 PETER 3:12 | *The eyes of the Lord watch over those who do right, and his ears are open to their prayers. But the Lord turns his face against those who do evil.*

God listens carefully to every prayer and answers it. His answer may be yes, no, or wait. Any loving parent gives all three of these responses to a child. God's answering yes to every request would spoil you and be dangerous to your well-being. Answering no to every request would be vindictive, stingy, and damaging to your spirit. Answering wait to every prayer would be frustrating. God always answers based on what he knows is best for you.

JAMES 5:16 | *The earnest prayer of a righteous person has great power and produces wonderful results.*

1 JOHN 5:14-15 | *He hears us whenever we ask for anything that pleases him. And . . . he will give us what we ask for.*

As you maintain a close relationship with Jesus and consistently study his Word, your prayers will be more aligned with his will. When that happens, God is delighted to grant your requests.

2 CORINTHIANS 12:8-9 | *Three different times [Paul] begged the Lord to take [the thorn in his flesh] away. Each time he said, "My grace is all you need. My power works best in weakness."*

Sometimes, like Paul, you will find that God answers prayer by giving you something better than you asked for.

EXODUS 14:15 | *The LORD said to Moses, "Why are you crying out to me? Tell the people to get moving!"*

Effective prayer is accompanied by a willingness to obey. When God opens a door, walk through it!

Promise from God PSALM 145:18 | *The LORD is close to all who call on him, yes, to all who call on him in truth.*

PREJUDICE

See also **DIFFERENCES, JUDGING OTHERS**

What does the Bible say about ethnic or racial prejudice?

LUKE 10:33 | *A despised Samaritan came along, and when he saw the man, he felt compassion for him.*

JOHN 4:9 | *The woman was surprised, for Jews refuse to have anything to do with Samaritans. She said to Jesus, "You are a Jew, and I am a Samaritan woman. Why are you asking me for a drink?"*

ACTS 10:28 | *Peter [said], "You know it is against our laws for a Jewish man to enter a Gentile home like this or to associate with you. But God has shown me that I should no longer think of anyone as impure or unclean."*

Jesus broke the judgmental stereotypes of his time. He reached across lines of racial and gender prejudice and division to demonstrate equality and respect for all people. God made us all different so that when we work together, our efforts are more complete and more effective for everyone. There are few things more powerful and productive than a diverse group of people working in unity.

What are other areas that can foster prejudice?

1 SAMUEL 16:7 | *The LORD said to Samuel, "Don't judge by his appearance or height. . . . The LORD doesn't see things the way you see them. People judge by outward appearance, but the LORD looks at the heart."*

ISAIAH 53:2 | *My servant grew up in the LORD's presence like a tender green shoot, like a root in dry ground. There was nothing beautiful or majestic about his appearance, nothing to attract us to him.*

Appearance. Stereotypes abound—prejudice against all kinds of people. But the real person is inside; the body is only the shell, the temporary housing. It is wrong to judge a person by outward appearance; the real person inside may be a person of incredible beauty. Even Jesus may not have had the tall, handsome body often attributed to him, for Isaiah the prophet said about the coming Savior, "There was nothing beautiful or majestic about his appearance."

PROVERBS 14:20-21 | *The poor are despised even by their neighbors, while the rich have many "friends." It is a sin to belittle one's neighbor; blessed are those who help the poor.*

JAMES 2:3-4 | *If you give special attention and a good seat to the rich person, but you say to the poor one, "You can stand over there, or else sit on the floor"—well, doesn't this discrimination show that your judgments are guided by evil motives?*

Economic status. Be careful that you don't show favoritism to a person who has more money than someone else.

MATTHEW 18:10 | *[Jesus said,] "Beware that you don't look down on any of these little ones. For I tell you that in heaven their angels are always in the presence of my heavenly Father."*

1 TIMOTHY 4:12 | *Don't let anyone think less of you because you are young.*

1 TIMOTHY 5:1 | *Never speak harshly to an older man, but appeal to him respectfully as you would to your own father.*

Age. To youth belongs the future; to old age belongs the honor of accomplishment. Youth has the opportunity to win the world; old age has the experience of victory. Each should be honored for its contributions.

MARK 6:2-3 | *[Those who heard Jesus' teaching] asked, "Where did he get all this wisdom and the power to perform such miracles?" Then they scoffed, "He's just a carpenter, the son of Mary. . . ." They were deeply offended and refused to believe in him.*

Occupation. God does not write off families or occupations, and perhaps that is why Jesus chose to come to the family of a carpenter rather than to the family of a king. God loves each person, regardless of occupation.

JOHN 1:46 | *"Nazareth!" exclaimed Nathanael. "Can anything good come from Nazareth?"*

Location. You must not be prejudiced because of where a person grew up. The "other side of the tracks" is often viewed negatively, but God lives on both sides of the tracks.

Promise from God COLOSSIANS 3:14 | *Above all, clothe your-selves with love, which binds us all together in perfect harmony.*

PREPARATION

How can I prepare for life's challenges?

NUMBERS 27:15-17 | *Moses said to the LORD, "O LORD, you are the God who gives breath to all creatures. Please appoint a new man as leader for the community. Give them someone who will guide them wherever they go and will lead them into battle, so the community of the LORD will not be like sheep without a shepherd."*

Anticipating what may be ahead often shows you what will need to be done when the moment arrives.

PROVERBS 4:23 | *Guard your heart above all else, for it determines the course of your life.*

The best time to prepare for temptation is before it presses in on you. Train yourself in the quieter times so that you will have the spiritual wisdom, strength, and commitment to honor God in the face of intense desires and temptation.

JOSHUA 3:5 | *Joshua told the people, "Purify yourselves, for tomorrow the LORD will do great wonders among you."*

2 TIMOTHY 2:21 | *If you keep yourself pure, you will be a special utensil for honorable use. Your life will be clean, and you will be ready for the Master to use you for every good work.*

Purity—the desire to keep your heart as clean as possible from sin—prepares your heart to be filled with God's wisdom and guidance so that you can serve him better and be involved in the work he is doing around you.

Promise from God MATTHEW 25:34 | *The King will say to those on his right, "Come, you who are blessed by my Father, inherit the Kingdom prepared for you from the creation of the world."*

PRESSURE

See also **STRESS**

What are some of the dangers of pressure?

LUKE 10:40-41 | *Martha was distracted by the big dinner she was preparing. She came to Jesus and said, "Lord, doesn't it seem unfair to you that my sister just sits here while I do all the work? Tell her to come and help me." But the Lord said to her, "My dear Martha, you are worried and upset over all these details!"*

MATTHEW 13:22 | *The seed that fell among the thorns represents those who hear God's word, but all too quickly the message is crowded out by the worries of this life and the lure of wealth, so no fruit is produced.*

Pressure can cause us to focus on the unimportant and miss the important. As pressure squeezes our perspective inward, we lose our perspective outward. Preoccupation with the trivia of the moment blinds us to the big picture.

MARK 14:38 | *Keep watch and pray, so that you will not give in to temptation. For the spirit is willing, but the body is weak.*

Pressure often makes us vulnerable and weakens our resistance to temptation.

1 KINGS 11:4 | *In Solomon's old age, they turned his heart to worship other gods instead of being completely faithful to the LORD his God, as his father, David, had been.*

Pressure can make us rationalize sin and compromise our beliefs. The pressure of the seduction of riches may so occupy our hearts that we leave no room for God. Lust crowds out true love, whether in our relationship with our spouse or with God.

PSALM 6:7 | *My vision is blurred by grief; my eyes are worn out because of all my enemies.*

PSALM 77:2-3 | *When I was in deep trouble, I searched for the Lord. All night long I prayed, with hands lifted toward heaven, but my soul was not comforted. I think of God, and I moan, overwhelmed with longing for his help.*

Pressure can have negative physical effects. The mind, soul, and body are interrelated. As one malfunctions, the others may get out of sync. Spiritual distress can induce physical or mental distress, just as physical or mental distress can induce sickness in our soul.

Is pressure ever positive?

JAMES 1:2-4 | *Dear brothers and sisters, when troubles come your way, consider it an opportunity for great joy. For you know that when your faith is tested, your endurance has a chance to grow. So let it grow, for when your endurance is fully developed, you will be perfect and complete, needing nothing.*

ROMANS 5:3 | *We can rejoice, too, when we run into problems and trials, for we know that they help us develop endurance.*

2 CHRONICLES 32:31 | *However, when ambassadors arrived from Babylon to ask about the remarkable events that had taken place in the land, God withdrew from Hezekiah in order to test him and to see what was really in his heart.*

Pressure can test and develop strength of character. The question is not whether we will have pressure, but what we will do with pressure when it comes. If we deal with pressure with our own strength, we may be quickly and easily overcome. If we let God help us deal with our pressure, we can come out stronger and more joyful.

ECCLESIASTES 12:11 | *The words of the wise are like cattle prods—painful but helpful.*

The pressure to learn can be positive, equipping you for the future.

How can I best handle pressure?

MARK 14:35-36 | *[Jesus] went on a little farther and fell to the ground. He prayed that, if it were possible, the awful hour awaiting him might pass him by. "Abba, Father," he cried out, "everything is possible for you. Please take this cup of suffering away from me. Yet I want your will to be done, not mine."*

Consider following Jesus' example of praying to God, seeking support from others, and focusing on God's will.

MATTHEW 4:10 | *"Get out of here, Satan," Jesus told him. "For the Scriptures say, 'You must worship the LORD your God and serve only him.'"*

PSALM 119:143 | *As pressure and stress bear down on me, I find joy in your commands.*

Immerse yourself in and obey God's Word. The more you find joy in the Lord, the less you will feel stress from external pressures.

EXODUS 18:17-18, 24 | *"This is not good!" Moses' father-in-law exclaimed. "You're going to wear yourself out—and the people, too. This job is too heavy a burden for you to handle all by yourself."* . . . *Moses listened to his father-in-law's advice and followed his suggestions.*

Listen to wise counsel. Delegation is often an overlooked solution to the mounting pressure you feel from trying to do everything yourself.

DANIEL 3:14, 16-18 | *Nebuchadnezzar said to them, "Is it true, Shadrach, Meshach, and Abednego, that you refuse to serve my gods or to worship the gold statue I have set up?"* . . . *Shadrach, Meshach, and Abednego replied, "O Nebuchadnezzar, we do not need to defend ourselves before you. If we are thrown into the blazing furnace, the God whom we serve is able to save us. He will rescue us from your power, Your Majesty. But even if he doesn't, we want to make it clear to you, Your Majesty, that we will never serve your gods or worship the gold statue you have set up."*

GENESIS 39:10, 12 | *She kept putting pressure on Joseph day after day, but he refused to sleep with her, and he kept out of her way as much as possible.* . . . *She came and grabbed him by his cloak, demanding, "Come on, sleep with me!" Joseph tore himself away . . . [and] ran from the house.*

The pressure you feel from temptation to sin can best be handled by acknowledging sin as sin and standing firm.

Standing firm sometimes means physically fleeing from things that bring oppressive pressures.

MATTHEW 11:28-30 | *Then Jesus said, "Come to me, all of you who are weary and carry heavy burdens, and I will give you rest. Take my yoke upon you. Let me teach you, because I am humble and gentle at heart, and you will find rest for your souls. For my yoke is easy to bear, and the burden I give you is light."*

1 PETER 5:7 | *Give all your worries and cares to God, for he cares about you.*

Prayerfully enjoy the peace of knowing that God is in control.

How can I resist negative peer pressure?

JAMES 4:17 | *Remember, it is sin to know what you ought to do and then not do it.*

1 CORINTHIANS 10:13 | *The temptations in your life are no different from what others experience. And God is faithful. He will not allow the temptation to be more than you can stand. When you are tempted, he will show you a way out so that you can endure.*

Look for God's way out in every tempting situation. God's way may take you away from, around, above, or through the temptation, but it will get you safely to the other side.

EXODUS 23:2 | *You must not follow the crowd in doing wrong. When you are called to testify in a dispute, do not be swayed by the crowd to twist justice.*

PROVERBS 24:1 | *Don't envy evil people or desire their company.*

The best way to resist negative peer pressure is to choose wise peers.

MATTHEW 1:20, 24 | *As he considered this, an angel of the Lord appeared to him in a dream. "Joseph, son of David," the angel said, "do not be afraid to take Mary as your wife. For the child within her was conceived by the Holy Spirit." . . . When Joseph woke up, he did as the angel of the Lord commanded and took Mary as his wife.*

Determine to obey God no matter what others may think. What God thinks of you is infinitely more important than what others think of you.

MATTHEW 14:9 | *Then the king regretted what he had said; but because of the vow he had made in front of his guests, he issued the necessary orders.*

Never let your pride or the risk of embarrassment keep you from making right choices.

How can I help others who are under pressure?

PHILIPPIANS 2:4 | *Don't look out only for your own interests, but take an interest in others, too.*

You can avoid becoming so preoccupied with your own pressures that you become insensitive to the pressure others face. Often as you help others with their pressures, you may relieve your own.

1 CORINTHIANS 8:9 | *You must be careful so that your freedom does not cause others with a weaker conscience to stumble.*

Don't allow your lifestyle to create additional pressures for others.

HEBREWS 10:24 | *Think of ways to motivate one another to acts of love and good works.*

PROVERBS 27:17 | *As iron sharpens iron, so a friend sharpens a friend.*

PROVERBS 12:25 | *Worry weighs a person down; an encouraging word cheers a person up.*

Be an encouragement to others who are under pressure.

Are there ways I can prevent—or minimize—pressure?

1 KINGS 22:13-14 | *Meanwhile, the messenger who went to get Micaiah said to him, "Look, all the prophets are promising victory for the king. Be sure that you agree with them and promise success." But Micaiah replied, "As surely as the LORD lives, I will say only what the LORD tells me to say."*

You can determine to be faithful to God before the time of pressure comes. Then you don't have to make that decision when you're under pressure.

PSALM 38:4 | *My guilt overwhelms me—it is a burden too heavy to bear.*

You can obey God, for meeting pressure his way will bring you peace.

1 CORINTHIANS 15:33 | *Don't be fooled by those who say such things, for "bad company corrupts good character."*

PSALM 1:1 | *Oh, the joys of those who do not follow the advice of the wicked, or stand around with sinners, or join in with mockers.*

You can respond to ungodly pressures better when you choose godly companions and counselors.

Promise from God PSALM 55:22 | *Give your burdens to the LORD, and he will take care of you. He will not permit the godly to slip and fall.*

PRIDE

See also **HUMILITY**

Why is pride considered one of the "seven deadly sins," even though other things seem so much worse?

EZEKIEL 28:17 | *Your heart was filled with pride because of all your beauty.*

The Bible indicates that pride was the sin that caused Lucifer (Satan) to be cast from heaven. If selfish pride is strong enough to rip an angel away from the very presence of God, it is certainly strong enough to cause damage in your own life.

PSALM 10:4 | *The wicked are too proud to seek God. They seem to think that God is dead.*

Pride leads to ignoring God and a life of disobedience.

2 TIMOTHY 3:2-4 | *People will love only themselves and their money. They will be boastful and proud. . . . They will be unloving and unforgiving. . . . They will betray their friends, be reckless, be puffed up with pride, and love pleasure rather than God.*

Pride can destroy relationships faster than almost anything else. It can cause you to elevate yourself at the expense of others.

2 CHRONICLES 26:16 | *When [Uzziah] had become powerful, he also became proud, which led to his downfall.*

An inflated estimation of your past successes leads to prideful behavior and ultimately to judgment.

OBADIAH 1:3 | *You have been deceived by your own pride because you live in a rock fortress and make your home high in the mountains.*

Pride finds comfort in false security.

Is pride ever healthy and appropriate?

ROMANS 15:17 | *[Paul said,] "I have reason to be enthusiastic about all Christ Jesus has done through me in my service to God."*

It is appropriate to feel satisfaction in what God does through you.

GALATIANS 6:14 | *As for me, may I never boast about anything except the cross of our Lord Jesus Christ.*

Pride is appropriate when it expresses itself in gratefulness to God for his gifts. When you look at your spouse or your children or your talents, and your heart wells up with gratitude to God, he is pleased. Then your focus is on him and not on yourself and your interests.

Promise from God PROVERBS 16:18 | *Pride goes before destruction, and haughtiness before a fall.*

PROBLEMS

See also **ADVERSITY, WORRY**

How does God view my problems?

1 PETER 5:7 | *Give all your worries and cares to God, for he cares about you.*

God cares about you and your problems.

PSALM 145:14 | *The LORD helps the fallen and lifts those bent beneath their loads.*

God is not only aware of your problems but wants to help you resolve them.

How can I anticipate problems and prepare for them?

JUDE 1:20-21 | *But you, dear friends, must build each other up in your most holy faith, pray in the power of the Holy Spirit, and await the mercy of our Lord Jesus Christ, who will bring you eternal life. In this way, you will keep yourselves safe in God's love.*

Realize that problems are inevitable; they will come. So the question is not "Will problems come?" but "What will I do with problems when they come?"

EPHESIANS 6:11-12 | *Put on all of God's armor so that you will be able to stand firm against all strategies of the devil. For we are not fighting against flesh-and-blood enemies, but against evil rulers and authorities of the unseen world, against mighty powers in this dark world, and against evil spirits in the heavenly places.*

You can best prepare for life's inevitable problems by living a life of faith, love, obedience, and prayer. You are encouraged to be strong with God's power. If you go onto life's battlefields already equipped with God's spiritual armor, you will more quickly and easily win the battles that your problems bring. The heat of battle is no time to be looking for armor and reading a manual about the way to use it.

How can I best cope with life's problems?

PHILIPPIANS 4:6 | *Don't worry about anything; instead, pray about everything. Tell God what you need, and thank him for all he has done.*

PSALM 56:3-4 | *When I am afraid, I will put my trust in you. I praise God for what he has promised. I trust in God, so why should I be afraid? What can mere mortals do to me?*

ISAIAH 26:3 | *You will keep in perfect peace all who trust in you, all whose thoughts are fixed on you!*

God is your first and primary point of confidence and trust as you communicate with him honestly about your worries and fears. At times your problems are just too big for you. So you need someone bigger, wiser, and stronger than you or your problems to help, and that is God.

PSALM 119:24 | *Your laws please me; they give me wise advice.*

GALATIANS 6:2 | *Share each other's burdens, and in this way obey the law of Christ.*

EXODUS 18:19, 24 | *"Now listen to me, and let me give you a word of advice, and may God be with you." . . . . Moses listened to his father-in-law's advice and followed his suggestions.*

Godly people can be a source of godly counsel.

ACTS 16:22-25 | *A mob quickly formed against Paul and Silas, and the city officials ordered them stripped and beaten with wooden rods. They were severely beaten, and then they were thrown into prison. The jailer was ordered to make sure they didn't escape. So the jailer put them into the inner dungeon and clamped their feet in the stocks. Around midnight Paul and Silas were praying and singing hymns to God, and the other prisoners were listening.*

JAMES 1:2 | *When troubles come your way, consider it an opportunity for great joy.*

Your problems do not have to weaken your faith, praise, or joy. Seeking God's solutions for your problems can enhance your faith, praise, and joy.

How should I learn and grow from my problems?

PSALM 107:43 | *Those who are wise will take all this to heart; they will see in our history the faithful love of the LORD.*

The more you see God at work in your problems, the more you learn about his faithful, loving character in your life. The more you learn about what God does, the more you will want to learn about who he is.

JAMES 1:3-4, 12 | *When your faith is tested, your endurance has a chance to grow. So let it grow, for when your endurance is fully developed, you will be perfect and complete, needing nothing. . . . God blesses those who patiently endure testing.*

The more you endure life's problems, the more you see your own character strengthened. The more you become the kind of person God desires, the more you can do the kind of work God desires.

PHILIPPIANS 4:12-13 | *I have learned the secret of living in every situation, whether it is with a full stomach or empty, with plenty or little. For I can do everything through Christ, who gives me strength.*

2 CORINTHIANS 1:8-9 | *We were crushed and overwhelmed beyond our ability to endure, and we thought we would never live through it. In fact, we expected to die. But as a result, we stopped relying on ourselves and learned to rely only on God, who raises the dead.*

The more you endure life's problems, the more you learn the source of your strength and your help. Don't hesitate to turn to God for strength.

How can I help others in the midst of their problems?

HEBREWS 13:1-2 | *Keep on loving each other as brothers and sisters. Don't forget to show hospitality to strangers, for some who have done this have entertained angels without realizing it!*

PHILIPPIANS 4:14 | *Even so, you have done well to share with me in my present difficulty.*

OBADIAH 1:12 | *You should not have gloated when they exiled your relatives to distant lands. You should not have rejoiced when the people of Judah suffered such misfortune. You should not have spoken arrogantly in that terrible time of trouble.*

2 CORINTHIANS 1:3-4 | *All praise to God, the Father of our Lord Jesus Christ. God is our merciful Father and the source of all comfort. He comforts us in all our troubles so that we can comfort others. When they are troubled, we will be able to give them the same comfort God has given us.*

You can genuinely love others with your actions, your emotions, your attitudes, your words, and your presence. Love resolves a thousand problems and prevents a thousand more.

Promise from God   PHILIPPIANS 4:6 | *Don't worry about anything; instead, pray about everything. Tell God what you need, and thank him for all he has done.*

PROTECTION

Does God protect those who love him from physical harm?

PSALM 91:11 | *[The Lord] will order his angels to protect you wherever you go.*

DANIEL 6:22 | *My God sent his angel to shut the lions' mouths so that they would not hurt me.*

Sometimes God protects and delivers you in miraculous ways in order to preserve you so you can continue to serve him.

2 CORINTHIANS 12:7 | *[Paul said,] "I was given a thorn in my flesh, a messenger from Satan to torment me and keep me from becoming proud."*

Sometimes, like Paul, you may experience devastating physical hardship and suffering. These are the times when your faith is put to the test.

ROMANS 5:3-4 | *We can rejoice, too, when we run into problems and trials, for we know that they help us develop endurance. And endurance develops strength of character.*

When God does not prevent suffering, he promises strength through the Holy Spirit to endure. Enduring suffering may bring you closer to God than being spared from suffering.

If I have an accident, a tragedy, or illness, does it mean God is punishing me for something?

JOHN 9:2-3 | *His disciples asked [Jesus], "Why was this man born blind? Was it because of his own sins or his parents' sins?" "It was not because of his sins or his parents' sins," Jesus answered. "This happened so the power of God could be seen in him."*

God is the redeemer of your suffering and not the cause. Suffering can take you toward God or away from him. If suffering takes you toward God, it is redemptive.

If God doesn't guarantee physical safety, what's the point of faith?

PSALM 23:4 | *Even when I walk through the darkest valley, I will not be afraid, for you are close beside me. Your rod and your staff protect and comfort me.*

JOHN 10:27-29 | *[Jesus said,] "My sheep listen to my voice; I know them, and they follow me. I give them eternal life, and they will never perish. No one can snatch them away from me, for my Father has given them to me, and he is more powerful than anyone else. No one can snatch them from the Father's hand."*

Faith has more to do with the eternal safety of your soul than the physical safety of your body.

2 TIMOTHY 1:12 | *I know the one in whom I trust, and I am sure that he is able to guard what I have entrusted to him until the day of his return.*

Faith is trusting God to guard and keep that which is eternal— your soul.

Is it wrong to pray for safety for myself and my loved ones?

ACTS 12:5 | *While Peter was in prison, the church prayed very earnestly for him.*

God always welcomes the expression of your desires when offered in submission to his will.

ROMANS 1:10 | *[Paul said,] "One of the things I always pray for is the opportunity, God willing, to come at last to see you."*

Paul's prayer for safety in travel was rooted in his desire to minister to others.

2 CORINTHIANS 1:11 | *You are helping us by praying for us. Then many people will give thanks because God has graciously answered so many prayers for our safety.*

The early apostles depended on the prayers for safety offered by the churches.

Promise from God PSALM 34:7 | *The angel of the LORD is a guard; he surrounds and defends all who fear him.*

REGRETS

See also **FORGIVENESS**

How can I deal with regrets in my life?

2 CORINTHIANS 5:17 | *Anyone who belongs to Christ has become a new person. The old life is gone; a new life has begun!*

PHILIPPIANS 3:13 | *I focus on this one thing: Forgetting the past and looking forward to what lies ahead.*

Focus on God, who controls the future, not on regrets of the past.

MATTHEW 16:18 | *[Jesus said,] "Now I say to you that you are Peter (which means 'rock'), and upon this rock I will build my church, and all the powers of hell will not conquer it."*

MATTHEW 26:73-75 | *Some of the other bystanders came over to Peter and said, "You must be one of them; we can tell by your Galilean accent." Peter swore, "A curse on me if I'm lying—I don't know the man!" And immediately the rooster crowed. Suddenly, Jesus' words flashed through Peter's mind: "Before the rooster crows, you will deny three times that you even know me." And he went away, weeping bitterly.*

GALATIANS 2:7-9 | *God had given . . . Peter the responsibility of preaching to the Jews. . . . God . . . worked through Peter as the apostle to the Jews. . . . In fact, James, Peter, and John . . . were known as pillars of the church.*

Turn your regrets into resolve. Regrets can be so powerful that they disable you. Don't let regret paralyze you; instead, let it motivate you to positive action.

ROMANS 8:28 | *God causes everything to work together for the good of those who love God and are called according to his purpose for them.*

Remember that God has the ability to turn bad into good. He can use even the things you regret to accomplish his will.

1 CHRONICLES 21:8 | *David said to God, "I have sinned greatly by taking this census. Please forgive my guilt for doing this foolish thing."*

MATTHEW 18:21-22 | *Peter came to [Jesus] and asked, "Lord, how often should I forgive someone who sins against me? Seven times?" "No, not seven times," Jesus replied, "but seventy times seven!"*

LUKE 15:18 | *I will go home to my father and say, "Father, I have sinned against both heaven and you."*

Sin always brings regret because it damages the relationships most important to you. Whether you were in the wrong or someone else wronged you, there is now a deep rift in a relationship; now you are facing conflict, separation, loneliness, frustration, anger, and other kinds of emotions. Forgiveness—whether confessing your wrongdoing to God and others or granting forgiveness to others—is the only way to give your heart a chance to start over. It doesn't take away past regrets, but it changes your perspective from regret to restoration. It keeps you focused on the healing that can happen in the future rather than on the wounds that you caused (or received) in the past.

How can I avoid regrets?

MATTHEW 7:12 | *Do to others whatever you would like them to do to you. This is the essence of all that is taught in the law and the prophets.*

When you treat others the way you like to be treated, you will have no regrets.

2 CORINTHIANS 1:12 | *We can say with confidence and a clear conscience that we have lived with a God-given holiness and sincerity in all our dealings.*

1 PETER 3:15-17 | *You must worship Christ as Lord of your life. And if someone asks about your Christian hope, always be ready to explain it. But do this in a gentle and respectful way. Keep your conscience clear. Then if people speak against you, they will be ashamed when they see what a good life you live because you belong to Christ. Remember, it is better to suffer for doing good, if that is what God wants, than to suffer for doing wrong!*

Follow your conscience and always do what is right. This will keep you from getting into situations you will later regret.

MATTHEW 27:3 | *When Judas, who had betrayed [Jesus], realized that Jesus had been condemned to die, he was filled with remorse.*

Thinking through the full consequences of your decisions in advance will keep you from making decisions you will later regret.

1 THESSALONIANS 5:22 | *Stay away from every kind of evil.*

Stay away from the places and people who tempt you to do wrong, and you will have less to regret.

PSALM 1:1-2 | *Oh, the joys of those who do not follow the advice of the wicked, or stand around with sinners, or join in with mockers. But they delight in the law of the LORD, meditating on it day and night.*

Surround yourself with positive influences who will give you good advice.

PROVERBS 14:29 | *People with understanding control their anger; a hot temper shows great foolishness.*

Avoid acting on impulse in the heat of anger. A hasty mistake has lasting effects.

EXODUS 23:2-3 | *Do not be swayed by the crowd to twist justice. And do not slant your testimony in favor of a person.*

Don't let your peers pressure you into doing something you know is foolish or wrong.

PROVERBS 15:1 | *A gentle answer deflects anger, but harsh words make tempers flare.*

JAMES 3:2, 5 | *If we could control our tongues, we . . . could also control ourselves in every other way. . . . The tongue is a small thing that makes grand speeches. But a tiny spark can set a great forest on fire.*

The greatest regrets are often caused by words; once spoken, they cannot be taken back. If you have even a hint that you might regret what you are about to say, don't speak.

Promise from God 2 CORINTHIANS 7:10 | *The kind of sorrow God wants us to experience leads us away from sin and results in salvation. There's no regret for that kind of sorrow.*

REPUTATION

See also **CHARACTER**

How can I cultivate and maintain a godly reputation?

PROVERBS 3:1-2 | *Never forget the things I have taught you. Store my commands in your heart. If you do this, . . . your life will be satisfying.*

Following God's direction in Scripture is the essential ingredient in developing a godly reputation.

PROVERBS 3:3-4 | *Never let loyalty and kindness leave you! Tie them around your neck as a reminder. Write them deep within your heart. Then you will find favor with both God and people, and you will earn a good reputation.*

God promises to give you a good name when you show kindness, loyalty, and love to people.

PROVERBS 22:1 | *Choose a good reputation over great riches; being held in high esteem is better than silver or gold.*

God blesses your reputation when you resist the temptation to trade your good name and honor for wealth.

ROMANS 14:17-18 | *The Kingdom of God is not a matter of what we eat or drink, but of living a life of goodness and peace and joy in the Holy Spirit. If you serve Christ with this attitude, you will please God, and others will approve of you, too.*

PHILIPPIANS 4:4-5 | *Always be full of joy in the Lord. I say it again—rejoice! Let everyone see that you are considerate in all you do.*

Focusing less on insignificant, external behaviors and more on internal character will please God, and ultimately will gain you the approval of others, too.

GALATIANS 5:22-23 | *The Holy Spirit produces this kind of fruit in our lives: love, joy, peace, patience, kindness, goodness, faithfulness, gentleness, and self-control.*

People often argue that their personal lives do not matter as long as they perform well on the job or look good in public.

God, however, does not make a distinction between public and private life. Justice, righteousness, integrity, mercy, honesty, fairness, and faithfulness are essential traits of a person's character and reputation because they reflect God's character. You will have a good reputation when you display the same integrity in private as you do in public.

How can a bad reputation be changed?

1 PETER 2:11-12 | *Dear friends, I warn you as "temporary residents and foreigners" to keep away from worldly desires that wage war against your very souls. Be careful to live properly among your . . . neighbors. Then . . . they will see your honorable behavior, and they will give honor to God.*

The surest way to influence how others think of you is by consistent, honorable behavior.

ROMANS 12:2 | *Don't copy the behavior and customs of this world, but let God transform you into a new person by changing the way you think. Then you will learn to know God's will for you, which is good and pleasing and perfect.*

Jesus' love can transform you, and eventually your reputation will change too.

How can I keep from damaging the reputation of others?

PROVERBS 25:10 | *Others may accuse you of gossip, and you will never regain your good reputation.*

Refrain from gossip, which robs other people of their reputation by taking away their integrity. With a single sentence you can ruin the reputation of others. By gossiping, you will damage your reputation as well.

Promise from God PROVERBS 22:1 | *Choose a good reputation over great riches; being held in high esteem is better than silver or gold.*

RESPECT

How do I gain respect?

I KINGS 13:8 | *The man of God said to the king, "Even if you gave me half of everything you own, I would not go with you."*

MATTHEW 7:12 | *Do to others whatever you would like them to do to you.*

You gain respect in much the same way you give it—by treating others the way you would like to be treated, standing up for truth no matter what, and not compromising your character.

How can I show respect to others?

LUKE 10:33-34 | *A despised Samaritan came along, and when he saw the man, he felt compassion for him. Going over to him, the Samaritan soothed his wounds with olive oil and wine and bandaged them. Then he put the man on his own donkey and took him to an inn, where he took care of him.*

ROMANS 12:10 | *Love each other with genuine affection, and take delight in honoring each other.*

ROMANS 13:7 | *Give to everyone what you owe them . . . , and give respect and honor to those who are in authority.*

PHILIPPIANS 2:3 | *Don't be selfish; don't try to impress others. Be humble, thinking of others as better than yourselves.*

JAMES 2:1 | *My dear brothers and sisters, how can you claim to have faith in our glorious Lord Jesus Christ if you favor some people over others?*

Respect involves showing more concern for people than for agendas, thinking highly of others, building them up in love, and treating everyone with fairness and integrity.

Promise from God PSALM 112:6, 9 | *Those who are righteous will be long remembered. . . . Their good deeds will be remembered forever. They will have influence and honor.*

RESPONSIBILITY

See also **DUTY**

Why is responsibility an important character trait?

GENESIS 39:2-3 | *The LORD was with Joseph, so he succeeded in everything he did as he served in the home of his Egyptian master. Potiphar noticed this and realized that the LORD was with Joseph, giving him success in everything he did.*

GENESIS 41:41 | *Pharaoh said to Joseph, "I hereby put you in charge of the entire land of Egypt."*

Responsibility can open doors of opportunity. If you are responsible with what you are given, greater opportunities and more responsibility will come your way.

GALATIANS 6:5 | *We are each responsible for our own conduct.*

Responsibility is important because you will be held accountable for your own actions. You cannot blame others for what you choose to do.

What are some things for which I am responsible?

GENESIS 2:15 | *The LORD God placed the man in the Garden of Eden to tend and watch over it.*

PSALM 8:4-6 | *What are mere mortals that you should think about them . . . ? Yet you made them only a little lower than God. . . . You gave them charge of everything you made, putting all things under their authority.*

You are responsible for the care of God's creation.

GENESIS 43:8-9 | *Judah said to his father, "Send the boy with me, and we will be on our way. . . . I personally guarantee his safety. You may hold me responsible if I don't bring him back to you."*

You are responsible for keeping your promises.

EXODUS 21:19 | *If he is later able to walk outside again, even with a crutch, the assailant will not be punished but must compensate his victim for lost wages and provide for his full recovery.*

You are responsible to compensate others for any injury or harm you cause them.

MATTHEW 12:37 | *The words you say will either acquit you or condemn you.*

You are responsible for the words you speak.

Promise from God MATTHEW 25:29 | *To those who use well what they are given, even more will be given, and they will* *have an abundance. But from those who do nothing, even what little they have will be taken away.*

SACRIFICE

What kinds of sacrifices am I called on to make?

HEBREWS 13:16 | *Don't forget to do good and to share with those in need. These are the sacrifices that please God.*

Just as Jesus gave himself for you, he wants you to give your-self in service to other people—even to the point of giving your life for them if necessary.

ROMANS 12:1 | *I plead with you to give your bodies to God because of all he has done for you. Let them be a living and holy sacri-fice—the kind he will find acceptable. This is truly the way to worship him.*

God wants you to give him your whole life, even if it means sacrificing comfort or pleasure.

EPHESIANS 5:2 | *Live a life filled with love, following the example of Christ. He loved us and offered himself as a sacrifice for us, a pleasing aroma to God.*

When you follow Jesus' example, it is pleasing to God.

Promise from God HEBREWS 9:28 | *Christ died once for all time as a sacrifice to take away the sins of many people. He will come again, not to deal with our sins, but to bring salvation to all who are eagerly waiting for him.*

SELF-CONTROL

See also **ACCOUNTABILITY, HABITS**

Why can't I seem to control certain desires?

ROMANS 7:21-25 | *I have discovered this principle of life—that when I want to do what is right, I inevitably do what is wrong. I love God's law with all my heart. But there is another power within me that is at war with my mind. This power makes me a slave to the sin that is still within me. Oh, what a miserable person I am! Who will free me from this life that is dominated by sin and death? Thank God! The answer is in Jesus Christ our Lord. So you see how it is: In my mind I really want to obey God's law, but because of my sinful nature I am a slave to sin.*

Because every person is born with a sinful nature, it will always be a struggle to do what is right and to not do what is wrong. Thankfully, God understands human weaknesses and gives each person the desire to please him. As you obey God, you will develop more self-control and the battle with your sinful nature will lessen.

ROMANS 12:1 | *Give your bodies to God because of all he has done for you. Let them be a living and holy sacrifice—the kind he will find acceptable. This is truly the way to worship him.*

You must truly want to give up the wrong desires you have.

What are some steps to exercising self-control?

PSALM 119:9 | *How can a . . . person stay pure? By obeying your word.*

2 TIMOTHY 2:5 | *Athletes cannot win the prize unless they follow the rules.*

To develop self-control, you first need to know God's guidelines for right living as found in the Bible. You need to know what you must control before you can keep it under control. Reading God's Word consistently—preferably every day—keeps his guidelines for right living fresh in your mind.

1 TIMOTHY 4:8 | *Physical training is good, but training for godliness is much better, promising benefits in this life and in the life to come.*

Self-control begins with God's work in you, but it requires your effort as well. Just as musicians and athletes must develop their talent, strength, and coordination through intentional effort, spiritual fitness must be intentional as well. God promises to reward such effort.

1 CORINTHIANS 10:13 | *The temptations in your life are no different from what others experience. And God is faithful. He will not allow the temptation to be more than you can stand. When you are tempted, he will show you a way out so that you can endure.*

You're not alone in your trials and temptations. Instead of thinking you have no hope for resisting, call on the Lord to lead you out of temptation. Ask trusted friends to keep you accountable. If you ask, God promises to give you what you need in order to resist.

PSALM 141:3 | *Take control of what I say, O LORD, and guard my lips.*

PROVERBS 13:3 | *Those who control their tongue will have a long life; opening your mouth can ruin everything.*

JAMES 1:26 | *If you claim to be religious but don't control your tongue, you are fooling yourself, and your religion is worthless.*

You exercise self-control by being careful of what you say. How often do you wish you could take back words as soon as they have left your mouth?

ROMANS 8:6 | *Letting your sinful nature control your mind leads to death. But letting the Spirit control your mind leads to life and peace.*

In order to have self-control, you must let God take control of your mind by fighting against the desires you know are wrong.

Promise from God JAMES 1:12 | *God blesses those who patiently endure testing and temptation. Afterward they will receive the crown of life that God has promised to those who love him.*

SELF-ESTEEM

See also **WORTH**

What makes me valuable?

ROMANS 8:15-17 | *You have not received a spirit that makes you fearful slaves. Instead, you received God's Spirit when he adopted you as his own children. Now we call him, "Abba, Father." For his Spirit joins with our spirit to affirm that we are God's children. And since we are his children, we are his heirs. In fact, together with Christ we are heirs of God's glory.*

People are tempted to measure their value on the basis of performance or other external measurements. But your worth is rooted in the fact that you are created in God's image and loved as God's child.

JEREMIAH 1:5 | *[The Lord said,] "I knew you before I formed you in your mother's womb. Before you were born I set you apart and appointed you as my prophet to the nations."*

God made you with great skill, crafting you with loving care. God showed how much value he places on you by the way he made you.

PSALM 139:1-3, 6 | *O LORD, you have examined my heart and know everything about me. You know when I sit down or stand up. You know my thoughts even when I'm far away. You see me when I travel and when I rest at home. You know everything I do. . . . Such knowledge is too wonderful for me.*

God values you so much that he watches over you no matter where you are or what you are doing.

How do I develop a healthy self-esteem?

ROMANS 12:3 | *Be honest in your evaluation of yourselves, measuring yourselves by the faith God has given us.*

Having a healthy self-esteem means having an honest appraisal of yourself, being not too proud because of the gifts and abilities God has given you, yet not so self-effacing that you fail to acknowledge and be grateful for your gifts and abilities.

1 PETER 4:10 | *God has given each of you a gift from his great variety of spiritual gifts. Use them well to serve one another.*

Giving actually increases your sense of self-worth because it allows God to work more effectively through you.

Promise from God   MATTHEW 10:29, 31 | *Not a single sparrow can fall to the ground without your Father knowing it. . . . You are more valuable to God than a whole flock of sparrows.*

SERVICE

The whole idea of service seems to run counter to what I was taught—to do my own thing. What does it mean to be a person who serves?

PHILIPPIANS 2:6-8 | *Though he was God, [Christ Jesus] did not think of equality with God as something to cling to. Instead, he gave up his divine privileges. . . . He humbled himself in obedience to God.*

A person who serves is humble and obedient to God.

MATTHEW 20:26-28 | *Whoever wants to be a leader among you must be your servant, and whoever wants to be first among you must become your slave. For even the Son of Man came not to be served but to serve others and to give his life as a ransom for many.*

A person who serves helps others regardless of their status in life.

JOHN 13:5 | *Then [Jesus] began to wash the disciples' feet, drying them with the towel he had around him.*

A person who serves gladly performs tasks that others consider beneath them.

ROMANS 6:13 | *Give yourselves completely to God. . . . Use your whole body as an instrument to do what is right for the glory of God.*

A person who serves uses all his or her energy and talents for the benefit of God and others.

What do I need in order to serve God?

PSALM 2:11 | *Serve the LORD with reverent fear, and rejoice with trembling.*

A joyful heart and reverent awe of God.

PSALM 42:1-2 | *As the deer longs for streams of water, so I long for you, O God. I thirst for God, the living God.*

PSALM 119:59 | *I pondered the direction of my life, and I turned to follow your laws.*

A desire to please God and walk in his ways.

MATTHEW 6:24 | *No one can serve two masters. For you will hate one and love the other; you will be devoted to one and despise the other.*

Loyalty to God.

ROMANS 7:6 | *Now we can serve God, not in the old way of obeying the letter of the law, but in the new way of living in the Spirit.*

A desire to be led by the Holy Spirit.

ACTS 20:19 | *I have done the Lord's work humbly and with many tears. I have endured the trials that came to me.*

Humility.

GALATIANS 5:13 | *You have been called to live in freedom, my brothers and sisters. But don't use your freedom to satisfy your sinful nature. Instead, use your freedom to serve one another in love.*

Love for others.

How can I serve others the best way possible?

MATTHEW 25:23 | *You have been faithful in handling this small amount, so now I will give you many more responsibilities.*

Demonstrate love and kindness to all people, especially those in need. Regardless of the level of your gifts and abilities, God expects you to invest what he's given you into the lives of others.

ROMANS 12:11 | *Never be lazy, but work hard and serve the Lord enthusiastically.*

Serve with enthusiasm and your attitude will not only energize you, it will also rub off on others.

Promise from God JOHN 15:10-12 | *[Jesus said,] "When you obey my commandments, you remain in my love. . . . I have told you these things so that you will be filled with my joy. Yes, your joy will overflow! This is my commandment: Love each other in the same way I have loved you."*

STRENGTHS/WEAKNESSES

How do I discover my strengths and weaknesses?

DANIEL 1:4 | *"Select only strong, healthy, and good-looking young men," [the king] said. "Make sure they are well versed in every branch of learning, are gifted with knowledge and good judgment, and are suited to serve in the royal palace. Train these young men in the language and literature of Babylon."*

Often your strengths are more evident to others than to yourself. Seek the advice of others to help you determine your strengths and weaknesses.

How can I take full advantage of my strengths and minimize my weaknesses?

ECCLESIASTES 4:12 | *A person standing alone can be attacked and defeated, but two can stand back-to-back and conquer. Three are even better, for a triple-braided cord is not easily broken.*

Join with others to help you minimize your weaknesses and maximize your strengths.

ECCLESIASTES 10:10 | *Using a dull ax requires great strength, so sharpen the blade. That's the value of wisdom; it helps you succeed.*

God can give you wisdom to know how to more fully develop your strengths.

1 CORINTHIANS 4:7 | *What do you have that God hasn't given you? And if everything you have is from God, why boast as though it were not a gift?*

Remember to give God credit for whatever strengths you have.

JEREMIAH 20:11 | *The LORD stands beside me like a great warrior. Before him my persecutors will stumble. They cannot defeat me.*

2 CORINTHIANS 12:9 | *[The Lord] said, "My grace is all you need. My power works best in weakness." So now I am glad to boast about my weaknesses, so that the power of Christ can work through me.*

God will stand beside you and give you strength when you are weak. Dedicate your weaknesses as well as your strengths to serving him.

Promise from God EPHESIANS 3:20 | *All glory to God, who is able, through his mighty power at work within us, to accomplish infinitely more than we might ask or think.*

STRESS

See also **BALANCE, PRESSURE**

What are some of the dangers of stress?

NUMBERS 11:10-11, 13-15 | *Moses was . . . very aggravated. And Moses said to the LORD, "Why are you treating me, your servant, so harshly? . . . What did I do to deserve the burden of all these people? . . . Where am I supposed to get meat for all these people? They keep whining to me, saying, 'Give us meat to eat!' I can't carry all these people by myself! The load is far too heavy! If this is how you intend to treat me, just go ahead and kill me. Do me a favor and spare me this misery!"*

2 CORINTHIANS 1:8 | *We think you ought to know, dear brothers and sisters, about the trouble we went through in the province of Asia. We were crushed and overwhelmed beyond our ability to endure, and we thought we would never live through it.*

The intense demands of life have the potential to overwhelm you. The expectations, as well as the scope of the need and the responsibility, are threats to even the strongest person.

MATTHEW 13:22 | *The seed that fell among the thorns represents those who hear God's word, but all too quickly the message is crowded out by the worries of this life.*

LUKE 10:40-41 | *Martha was distracted by the big dinner she was preparing. She came to Jesus and said, "Lord, doesn't it seem unfair to you that my sister just sits here while I do all the work? Tell her to come and help me." But the Lord said to her, "My dear Martha, you are worried and upset over all these details!"*

Stress can cause you to focus on the trivial and miss the important. As pressure squeezes your perspective inward, you lose the big picture. Preoccupation with the issues of the moment blinds you to what's really important.

How can I deal with stress?

2 CORINTHIANS 4:9 | *We are hunted down, but never abandoned by God. We get knocked down, but we are not destroyed.*

Keep going! Knowing that God is by your side during times of trouble and stress can help you to not give up.

PSALM 55:22 | *Give your burdens to the LORD, and he will take care of you.*

MATTHEW 11:28 | *Jesus said, "Come to me, all of you who are weary and carry heavy burdens, and I will give you rest."*

God's availability and promises are the most effective stress reducers of all.

2 SAMUEL 22:7 | *In my distress I cried out to the LORD. . . . He heard me from his sanctuary; my cry reached his ears.*

PSALM 86:7 | *I will call to you whenever I'm in trouble, and you will answer me.*

Be persistent in prayer.

MARK 6:31 | *Jesus said, "Let's go off by ourselves to a quiet place and rest awhile." He said this because there were so many people coming and going that Jesus and his apostles didn't even have time to eat.*

Take time to slow down and take a break from pressure-packed situations.

1 CORINTHIANS 6:19-20 | *Don't you realize that your body is the temple of the Holy Spirit, who lives in you and was given to you by God? You do not belong to yourself, for God bought you with a high price. So you must honor God with your body.*

Take care of your body. Adequate rest, regular exercise, and proper nutrition are essential to dealing effectively with stress.

GALATIANS 6:9 | *Let's not get tired of doing what is good. At just the right time we will reap a harvest of blessing if we don't give up.*

Don't let stress defeat you. When you are tired of doing good, you may be just too tired.

ISAIAH 41:10 | *Don't be afraid, for I am with you. Don't be discouraged, for I am your God. I will strengthen you and help you. I will hold you up with my victorious right hand.*

Turn from fear and anxiety to faith and peace. God promises to supply the power to get you through the hard times.

Is stress ever positive?

ROMANS 5:3-4 | *We can rejoice, too, when we run into problems and trials, for we know that they help us develop endurance. And endurance develops strength of character, and character strengthens our confident hope of salvation.*

JAMES 1:2-4 | *Dear brothers and sisters, when troubles come your way, consider it an opportunity for great joy. For you know that when your faith is tested, your endurance has a chance to grow. So let it grow, for when your endurance is fully developed, you will be perfect and complete, needing nothing.*

Stress and pressure can both test and develop strength of character. The question is not whether or not you will have stress, but what you will do with it when it comes. If you deal with stress and pressure in your own strength, you may be quickly and easily overcome. If you let God help you deal with your pressure, you can come out stronger and more joyful.

Promise from God   JOHN 16:33 | *I have told you all this so that you may have peace in me. Here on earth you will have many trials and sorrows. But take heart, because I have overcome the world.*

SUCCESS

See also **GOALS**

What is true success in God's eyes?

MATTHEW 22:37 | *Jesus [said], "You must love the LORD your God with all your heart, all your soul, and all your mind."*

JOHN 15:8 | *[Jesus said,] "When you produce much fruit, you are my true disciples. This brings great glory to my Father."*

Success is knowing God and living in a way that pleases him.

MATTHEW 20:25-26 | *Rulers in this world lord it over their people, and officials flaunt their authority over those under them. But among you it will be different. Whoever wants to be a leader among you must be your servant.*

Serving and helping others brings success, for in serving others you find true joy.

JOHN 15:8, 16 | *When you produce much fruit, you are my true disciples. This brings great glory to my Father. . . . You didn't choose me. I chose you. I appointed you to go and produce lasting fruit, so that the Father will give you whatever you ask for, using my name.*

Success is being productive—producing results that matter to God.

PROVERBS 16:3 | *Commit your actions to the LORD, and your plans will succeed.*

Committing all you do to God is success. When you put God first in your life, you can fully understand what is really important in life.

Promise from God PSALM 60:12 | *With God's help we will do mighty things.*

TEAMWORK

See also **DELEGATION**

What are some of the keys to successful teamwork?

AMOS 3:3 | *Can two people walk together without agreeing on the direction?*

NEHEMIAH 2:17-18 | *I said to them, "You know very well what trouble we are in. Jerusalem lies in ruins, and its gates have been destroyed by fire. Let us rebuild the wall of Jerusalem and end this disgrace!" Then I told them about how the gracious hand of God had been on me, and about my conversation with the king. They replied at once, "Yes, let's rebuild the wall!" So they began the good work.*

Making sure that everyone is "on the same page" regarding the vision and goals of the team is essential to seamless teamwork.

1 CORINTHIANS 1:10 | *Be of one mind, united in thought and purpose.*

PHILIPPIANS 2:2 | *Make me truly happy by agreeing whole-heartedly with each other, loving one another, and working together with one mind and purpose.*

LUKE 5:18-19 | *Some men came carrying a paralyzed man on a sleeping mat. They tried to take him inside to Jesus, but they couldn't reach him because of the crowd. So they went up to the roof and took off some tiles. Then they lowered the sick man on his mat down into the crowd, right in front of Jesus.*

When a team combines determination with hard work, the likelihood of success increases.

NEHEMIAH 4:16, 21 | *Half my men worked while the other half stood guard with spears, shields, bows, and coats of mail. . . . We worked early and late, from sunrise to sunset. And half the men were always on guard.*

A team that cooperates well is also effective.

EXODUS 4:15-16 | *[The Lord said to Moses,] "I will be with both of you as you speak, and I will instruct you both in what to do. Aaron will be your spokesman to the people. He will be your mouthpiece, and you will stand in the place of God for him, telling him what to say."*

EXODUS 17:12-13 | *Moses' arms soon became so tired he could no longer hold them up. So Aaron and Hur found a stone for him to sit on. Then they stood on each side of Moses, holding up his hands. So his hands held steady until sunset. As a result, Joshua overwhelmed the army of Amalek in battle.*

Teamwork means being united in purpose and, when necessary, helping each other finish the job.

Promise from God ECCLESIASTES 4:9, 12 | *Two people are better off than one, for they can help each other succeed. . . . A person standing alone can be attacked and defeated, but two can stand back-to-back and conquer. Three are even better, for a triple-braided cord is not easily broken.*

THOUGHTS

How can I control my thoughts?

JOSHUA 1:8 | *Study this Book of Instruction continually. Meditate on it day and night so you will be sure to obey everything written in it. Only then will you prosper and succeed in all you do.*

PSALM 119:11 | *I have hidden your word in my heart, that I might not sin against you.*

1 TIMOTHY 4:13, 15 | *Focus on reading the Scriptures to the church, encouraging the believers, and teaching them. . . . Give your complete attention to these matters.*

God is pleased when you think about his Word. Study and think about God's Word continually until it fills your mind.

1 CHRONICLES 28:9 | *[David said,] "Solomon, my son, learn to know the God of your ancestors intimately. Worship and serve him with your whole heart and a willing mind. For the LORD sees every heart and knows every plan and thought. If you seek him, you will find him."*

MATTHEW 22:37 | *You must love the LORD your God with all your heart, all your soul, and all your mind.*

It pleases God when your thoughts are full of love for him.

MATTHEW 5:28 | *Anyone who even looks at a woman with lust has already committed adultery with her in his heart.*

MARK 7:20-23 | *Then [Jesus] added, "It is what comes from inside that defiles you. For from within, out of a person's heart, come evil thoughts, sexual immorality, theft, murder, adultery, greed, wickedness, deceit, lustful desires, envy, slander, pride, and foolishness. All these vile things come from within; they are what defile you."*

Don't allow your mind to dwell on sinful thoughts. Bad thoughts are bound to pop into your mind, but it's when you allow them to stay that you get in trouble. When bad thoughts come to mind, don't entertain them—immediately turn to God in prayer.

PSALM 19:14 | *May the words of my mouth and the meditation of my heart be pleasing to you, O LORD, my rock and my redeemer.*

PSALM 26:2 | *Put me on trial, LORD, and cross-examine me. Test my motives and my heart.*

PSALM 139:23 | *Search me, O God, and know my heart; test me and know my anxious thoughts.*

Ask God to help you have pure thoughts by inviting him to examine your mind and convict you whenever you are thinking wrong things.

PHILIPPIANS 4:8 | *Fix your thoughts on what is true, and honorable, and right, and pure, and lovely, and admirable. Think about things that are excellent and worthy of praise.*

Make a conscious effort to practice thinking good thoughts, just as you might practice some other skill. These thoughts might be about the good in your life that you can be thankful for, the good in others that you appreciate, the good that you might do for others, or the goodness of God in providing you with earthly blessings and promising you eternal life.

ROMANS 12:2 | *Don't copy the behavior and customs of this world, but let God transform you into a new person by changing the way you think. Then you will learn to know God's will for you, which is good and pleasing and perfect.*

Be prepared to let God radically change not only what you think about but the way you think.

Promise from God 1 CHRONICLES 29:17 | *I know, my God, that you examine our hearts and rejoice when you find integrity there.*

TIREDNESS

What do I have to watch out for when I'm tired?

GALATIANS 6:9 | *Let's not get tired of doing what is good. At just the right time we will reap a harvest of blessing if we don't give up.*

Being tired makes you more susceptible to discouragement, temptation, and sin and causes you to lose hope that things will change in the future.

PROVERBS 30:1-2 | *I am weary, O God; I am weary and worn out, O God. I am too stupid to be human, and I lack common sense.*

Being tired causes you to lose perspective. When you're weary is not a good time to try to make important decisions.

JOB 10:1 | *I am disgusted with my life. Let me complain freely. My bitter soul must complain.*

Being tired can cause you to say things you may later regret.

ECCLESIASTES 1:8 | *Everything is wearisome beyond description. No matter how much we see, we are never satisfied. No matter how much we hear, we are not content.*

Being tired can cause you to lose your vision and purpose.

PSALM 127:2 | *It is useless for you to work so hard from early morning until late at night . . . for God gives rest to his loved ones.*

Always being tired may mean you are trying to do too much. It may be time for you to slow down.

2 SAMUEL 17:1-2 | *Ahithophel urged Absalom, "Let me choose 12,000 men to start out after David tonight. I will catch up with him while he is weary and discouraged. He and his troops will panic, and everyone will run away. Then I will kill only the king."*

Weariness makes you vulnerable to your enemies. When your guard is down, it's easier for them to attack you.

Who can help me when I grow tired?

HABAKKUK 3:19 | *The Sovereign LORD is my strength! He makes me as surefooted as a deer, able to tread upon the heights.*

EPHESIANS 6:10 | *Be strong in the Lord and in his mighty power.*

When you are weary, tap into the Lord's power—it is not some fable or fairy tale, but real supernatural power from the One who created you and sustains you.

1 KINGS 19:5-8 | *As [Elijah] was sleeping, an angel touched him and told him, "Get up and eat!" . . . So he ate and drank and lay down again. Then the angel of the LORD came again and touched him and said, "Get up and eat some more, or the journey ahead will be too much for you." So he got up and ate and drank, and the food gave him enough strength to travel.*

You can help yourself by taking good care of your body:
exercise, rest, and eat nutritious meals. These activities
will help you overcome weariness. Poor nutrition or health
habits invite burnout.

ISAIAH 40:29-31 | *He gives power to the weak and strength to the*
powerless. Even youths will become weak and tired, and young
men will fall in exhaustion. But those who trust in the LORD will
find new strength. They will soar high on wings like eagles. They
will run and not grow weary. They will walk and not faint.

The Lord will give you renewed strength when you grow
weary. When you come to him in praise, he refreshes your
heart. When you come to him in prayer, he refreshes your soul.
When you come to him in solitude, he refreshes your body.
When you come to him in need, he refreshes your spirit. When
you come to him with thankfulness, he refreshes your perspective. Coming to God releases the burdens of life and draws
strength from him, the source of strength.

Promise from God MATTHEW 11:28 | *Jesus said, "Come to me,*
all of you who are weary and carry heavy burdens, and I will
give you rest."

TROUBLED TIMES

How should I respond when trouble comes?

PSALM 142:2 | *I pour out my complaints before him and tell him*
all my troubles.

Immediately go to God—in honesty and in faith. Ask him
to give you help, wisdom, and guidance.

PSALM 25:16-18 | *Turn to me and have mercy, for I am alone and in deep distress. My problems go from bad to worse. Oh, save me from them all! Feel my pain and see my trouble. Forgive all my sins.*

When trouble strikes, you need to honestly search your heart to see if the problem might be a result of your own wrongdoing. If it is, you need to ask God's help in dealing with it. If it isn't, you still have the benefit of drawing closer to God.

MATTHEW 6:34 | *Don't worry about tomorrow, for tomorrow will bring its own worries. Today's trouble is enough for today.*

Don't be overcome by worry. Borrowing troubles from tomorrow through worry can cause physical and emotional bankruptcy.

ECCLESIASTES 8:6 | *There is a time and a way for everything, even when a person is in trouble.*

Be open to options and look for God's creative solution.

GALATIANS 6:2 | *Share each other's burdens.*

Gain strength and support from family and friends.

What can I learn from my troubles? What good can come from times of trouble?

ROMANS 8:28 | *And we know that God causes everything to work together for the good of those who love God and are called according to his purpose for them.*

PSALM 107:43 | *Those who are wise will take all this to heart; they will see in our history the faithful love of the LORD.*

God is always working in your life. Although you may not see his plan or even his activity in the midst of trouble, you can trust his love for you.

1 PETER 1:6-7 | *Be truly glad. There is wonderful joy ahead, even though you have to endure many trials for a little while. These trials will show that your faith is genuine. It is being tested as fire tests and purifies gold—though your faith is far more precious than mere gold. So when your faith remains strong through many trials, it will bring you much praise and glory and honor on the day when Jesus Christ is revealed to the whole world.*

PROVERBS 24:10 | *If you fail under pressure, your strength is too small.*

Troubles can test your faith, proving it pure and strong.

2 CORINTHIANS 1:8-10 | *We think you ought to know, dear brothers and sisters, about the trouble we went through in the province of Asia. We were crushed and overwhelmed beyond our ability to endure, and we thought we would never live through it. In fact, we expected to die. But as a result, we stopped relying on ourselves and learned to rely only on God. . . . And he did rescue us from mortal danger, and he will rescue us again.*

Troubles can help you learn to rely on God.

2 CORINTHIANS 1:3-4, 6 | *God is our merciful Father and the source of all comfort. He comforts us in all our troubles so that we can comfort others. When they are troubled, we will be able to give them the same comfort God has given us. . . . For when we ourselves are comforted, we will certainly comfort you. Then you can patiently endure the same things we suffer.*

Times of trouble can prepare you to offer comfort to others in their times of trouble.

Promise from God   NAHUM 1:7 | *The LORD is good, a strong refuge when trouble comes. He is close to those who trust in him.*

TRUST

Why is trust a key in strong relationships?

LEVITICUS 6:2-4 | *Suppose one of you sins against your associate and is unfaithful to the LORD. Suppose you cheat . . . or you steal or commit fraud, . . . [then] you are guilty.*

PROVERBS 20:23 | *The LORD detests double standards; he is not pleased by dishonest scales.*

PROVERBS 25:19 | *Putting confidence in an unreliable person in times of trouble is like chewing with a broken tooth or walking on a lame foot.*

Mutual trust with family members, friends, or the people you work with strengthens and deepens relationships because you know that what they tell you is true and that they are always acting in your best interests out of love. You have total peace of mind about them—you are free to fully enjoy those relationships. Mistrust is unhealthy and painful in relationships because it causes you to constantly question the motives of others.

Promise from God   ISAIAH 26:3 | *You will keep in perfect peace all who trust in you, all whose thoughts are fixed on you!*

TRUTH

See also **HONESTY**

Why is telling the truth so important?

PROVERBS 12:19 | *Truthful words stand the test of time, but lies are soon exposed.*

LUKE 16:10 | *If you are faithful in little things, you will be faithful in large ones. But if you are dishonest in little things, you won't be honest with greater responsibilities.*

If you are truthful in even small matters, you will have the reputation of being an honest person.

EPHESIANS 4:25 | *Stop telling lies. Let us tell our neighbors the truth, for we are all parts of the same body.*

Telling the truth promotes good relationships.

MATTHEW 12:33 | *A tree is identified by its fruit. If a tree is good, its fruit will be good. If a tree is bad, its fruit will be bad.*

Honest dealings reveal an honest character. What you do reveals who you are.

PSALM 24:3-5 | *Who may climb the mountain of the LORD? Who may stand in his holy place? Only those whose hands and hearts are pure, who . . . never tell lies. They will receive the LORD's blessing and have a right relationship with God their savior.*

Telling the truth is necessary for a relationship with God.

ROMANS 12:3 | *Be honest in your evaluation of yourselves, measuring yourselves by the faith God has given us.*

Honestly evaluating your walk with the Lord allows you to continue growing in your faith.

1 TIMOTHY 1:19 | *Cling to your faith in Christ, and keep your conscience clear. For some people have deliberately violated their consciences; as a result, their faith has been shipwrecked.*

Always telling the truth keeps a clear conscience.

PROVERBS 11:3 | *Honesty guides good people; dishonesty destroys treacherous people.*

There is freedom in honesty because you never have to worry about getting tripped up. Dishonesty and deception are a form of bondage because you get trapped by your lies.

Promise from God PSALM 119:160 | *The very essence of your words is truth; all your just regulations will stand forever.*

UNITY

What is true unity?

ROMANS 12:4-5 | *Just as our bodies have many parts and each part has a special function, so it is with Christ's body. We are many parts of one body, and we all belong to each other.*

Unity is not the same as uniformity. Everyone has unique gifts and personalities. True unity is the celebration and appreciation of these differences to reach the common goal of serving God.

Why is unity important?

1 CORINTHIANS 1:10 | *I appeal to you, dear brothers and sisters, by the authority of our Lord Jesus Christ, to live in harmony with each other. Let there be no divisions in the church. Rather, be of one mind, united in thought and purpose.*

Unity allows you to share a sense of fellowship and devotion and to work together with a common purpose.

How can I help achieve unity?

ROMANS 15:5 | *May God, who gives this patience and encouragement, help you live in complete harmony with each other, as is fitting for followers of Christ Jesus.*

By working hard to develop the same kind of attitude Jesus had, one of patience and encouragement, of uniting, not dividing.

EPHESIANS 4:12-13 | *Equip God's people to do his work and build up the church, the body of Christ. This will continue until we all come to such unity in our faith and knowledge of God's Son that we will be mature in the Lord, measuring up to the full and complete standard of Christ.*

By exercising your God-given responsibility to build others up.

1 PETER 3:8 | *All of you should be of one mind. Sympathize with each other. Love each other as brothers and sisters. Be tenderhearted, and keep a humble attitude.*

By sympathizing with others.

EPHESIANS 4:2-3 | *Always be humble and gentle. Be patient with each other, making allowance for each other's faults because of your love. Make every effort to keep yourselves united in the Spirit, binding yourselves together with peace.*

By being humble, recognizing that everyone has a contribution to make.

COLOSSIANS 3:13-14 | *Make allowance for each other's faults, and forgive anyone who offends you. Remember, the Lord forgave you, so you must forgive others. Above all, clothe yourselves with love, which binds us all together in perfect harmony.*

By loving and forgiving others.

Does unity mean everyone has to agree?

1 CORINTHIANS 12:12, 18-21 | *The human body has many parts, but the many parts make up one whole body. So it is with the body of Christ. . . . And God has put each part just where he wants it. How strange a body would be if it had only one part! Yes, there are many parts, but only one body. The eye can never say to the hand, "I don't need you." The head can't say to the feet, "I don't need you."*

Unity does not mean that everyone's opinion has to be the same, or even that their goals are the same. God has created everyone different, which means there will be differences of opinion. But your common purpose should be the same—to serve and honor God. Unity is ruined when selfish interests take priority.

PSALM 34:14 | *Search for peace, and work to maintain it.*

EPHESIANS 4:11-13, 15-16 | *These are the gifts Christ gave to the church . . . to equip God's people to do his work and build up the church, the body of Christ. This will continue until we all come to such unity in our faith and knowledge of God's Son that we will be mature in the Lord. . . . We will speak the truth in love, growing in every way more and more like Christ. . . . He makes the whole body fit together perfectly. As each part does its own special work, it helps the other parts grow, so that the whole body is healthy and growing and full of love.*

Living peaceably with others does not mean avoiding conflict; it means handling conflict appropriately. Conflict handled poorly leads to fractured relationships. Avoiding conflict altogether leads to the same end because there is unresolved hurt or anger. When conflict arises, don't retaliate in anger but respond with love and patient endurance that leads to the resolution of the problem.

Promise from God GALATIANS 3:26-28 | *You are all children of God through faith in Christ Jesus. And all who have been united with Christ in baptism have put on Christ, like putting on new clothes. There is no longer Jew or Gentile, slave or free, male and female. For you are all one in Christ Jesus.*

VALOR

See also **COURAGE**

What is valor?

PSALM 112:1, 8 | *How joyful are those who fear the LORD and delight in obeying his commands. . . . They are confident and fearless and can face their foes triumphantly.*

Valor is personal bravery, a fearlessness that compels a person to act without hesitation, to put one's life on the line for the good and/or protection of others. As you face extreme danger, you dig deeply into the strongest part of your mind and spirit.

1 SAMUEL 17:32 | *"Don't worry about this Philistine," David told Saul. "I'll go fight him!"*

1 SAMUEL 17:47 | *[David said,] "The LORD rescues his people, but not with sword and spear. This is the LORD's battle, and he will give you to us!"*

One of the most familiar stories in the Bible is the one-on-one combat between the Philistine giant Goliath and a young shepherd named David. When David arrived at the battlefield, he wasn't wearing armor or carrying heavy weapons; he had been sent by his father to check on his brothers' welfare. What he saw was not a pretty sight; Goliath and the Philistine army had paralyzed the Israelites with fear. Hearing Goliath's God-defying taunts, David's fierce loyalty immediately rose to the surface. Though he was young and inexperienced, his fearlessness, drawn from divine strength, sealed a miraculous victory.

2 SAMUEL 23:8-12 | *These are the names of David's mightiest warriors. The first was Jashobeam . . . [who] once used his spear to kill 800 enemy warriors in a single battle. . . . Eleazar and David stood together against the Philistines when the entire Israelite army had fled. He killed Philistines until his hand was too tired to lift his sword. . . . One time the Philistines gathered at Lehi and attacked the Israelites in a field full of lentils. The Israelite army fled, but Shammah held his ground in the middle of the field and beat back the Philistines. So the LORD brought about a great victory.*

Of all the thousands of men that David led into battle, Jashobeam, Eleazar, and Shammah are singled out in Scripture for their outstanding gallantry; they belonged in an elite group. Each of them could have been awarded a medal of valor for spirited and conspicuous bravery.

Why should valor be honored?

2 SAMUEL 23:15-17 | *David remarked longingly to his men, "Oh, how I would love some of that good water from the well by the gate in Bethlehem." So the Three broke through the Philistine lines, drew some water from the well by the gate in Bethlehem, and brought it back to David. But he refused to drink it. Instead, he poured it out as an offering to the LORD. "The LORD forbid that I should drink this!" he exclaimed. "This water is as precious as the blood of these men who risked their lives to bring it to me."*

David was in a cave, taking refuge from the Philistine army that occupied Bethlehem and the surrounding area. When David expressed a desire for water from his hometown, three of his top men immediately responded. David was astounded when they returned; his wish had not been a command. Realizing the sacrifice that his men had made for him, David honored their actions by offering the water to God in gratitude for them.

Promise from God PSALM 56:9 | *My enemies will retreat when I call to you for help. This I know: God is on my side!*

VALUES

How do I assess my current values?

PROVERBS 30:8 | *First, help me never to tell a lie.*

ROMANS 1:29 | *Their lives became full of every kind of wickedness, sin, greed, hate, envy, murder, quarreling, deception, malicious behavior, and gossip.*

EPHESIANS 5:4 | *Obscene stories, foolish talk, and coarse jokes—these are not for you. Instead, let there be thankfulness to God.*

How do you view those things that the Bible calls sin, such as gossip, flattery, profanity, lying, and cheating? Do your ideas of right and wrong agree with what God's Word says?

MATTHEW 15:19 | *From the heart come evil thoughts, murder, adultery, all sexual immorality, theft, lying, and slander.*

If your actions don't regularly match up with what God says is right, maybe you're overdue for a heart checkup. You need a change of heart before you can change your behavior.

How can a person cultivate godly values?

GENESIS 39:8-9 | *Joseph refused. "Look," he told her, "my master trusts me with everything in his entire household. . . . He has held back nothing from me except you, because you are his wife. How could I do such a wicked thing? It would be a great sin against God."*

Refuse the kind of lifestyle choices that are worthless or dangerous to long-term well-being.

PSALM 15:1-2 | *Who may worship in your sanctuary, LORD? . . . Those who lead blameless lives and do what is right, speaking the truth from sincere hearts.*

MICAH 6:8 | *O people, the LORD has told you what is good, and this is what he requires of you: to do what is right, to love mercy, and to walk humbly with your God.*

MATTHEW 7:12 | *Do to others whatever you would like them to do to you. This is the essence of all that is taught in the law and the prophets.*

GALATIANS 5:22-23 | *The Holy Spirit produces this kind of fruit in our lives: love, joy, peace, patience, kindness, goodness, faithfulness, gentleness, and self-control. There is no law against these things!*

Godly living simply means valuing what God values. To have godly values, you need God living in you. He promises that when you ask him, he will send his Holy Spirit to live in you, helping you to value and to live out what is truly important.

How important is it to live a consistently moral life?

EXODUS 23:24 | *You must not worship the gods of these nations or serve them in any way or imitate their evil practices.*

PSALM 24:3-4 | *Who may climb the mountain of the LORD? Who may stand in his holy place? Only those whose hands and hearts are pure, who do not worship idols and never tell lies.*

PROVERBS 28:2 | *When there is moral rot within a nation, its government topples easily.*

Strong moral values are essential to the well-being of any society.

Promise from God ROMANS 5:3-5 | *We can rejoice, too, when we run into problems and trials, for we know that they help us develop endurance. And endurance develops strength of character, and character strengthens our confident hope of salvation. And this hope will not lead to disappointment. For we know how dearly God loves us, because he has given us the Holy Spirit to fill our hearts with his love.*

VISION

See also **FOCUS**

Why is vision an important trait?

PSALM 119:18 | *Open my eyes to see.*

EPHESIANS 3:20 | *All glory to God, who is able, through his mighty power at work within us, to accomplish infinitely more than we might ask or think.*

Vision is a picture of the future that gives a person a passion for something right now. Lack of vision is like trying to see underwater without a mask—everything is blurry, nothing makes sense, and you feel completely lost. If you want to have purpose, if you want to clearly see the way in life, if you want to be motivated to do something that counts, you need vision—a picture of where you would like to be at some point in the future.

ZECHARIAH 8:4-6 | *This is what the LORD of Heaven's Armies says: Once again old men and women will walk Jerusalem's streets with their canes and will sit together in the city squares. And the streets of the city will be filled with boys and girls at play. This is what the LORD of Heaven's Armies says: All this may seem impossible to you now, a small remnant of God's people. But is it impossible for me? says the LORD of Heaven's Armies.*

ZECHARIAH 8:9 | *This is what the LORD of Heaven's Armies says: Be strong and finish the task!*

Having a vision helps get things moving and get things done. The Temple in Jerusalem still needed to be rebuilt after long years of exile, but the people weren't motivated to finish it. God gave Zechariah a vision of the city of Jerusalem once again filled with joyful people, and that vision, in turn, motivated the people to complete their task. A person must envision goals that are doable and plan how to accomplish them.

ECCLESIASTES 1:8 | *Everything is wearisome beyond description. No matter how much we see, we are never satisfied. No matter how much we hear, we are not content.*

Living in a state of constant weariness can blur a person's vision and purpose. It is hard for someone to look ahead when he or she feels helpless to go on. That is where God comes in. Asking him for help to view life from his perspective is a request that he longs to grant.

Promise from God 1 CORINTHIANS 13:12 | *Now we see things imperfectly, like puzzling reflections in a mirror, but then we will see everything with perfect clarity.*

WAR

See also **PEACE**

What does God think of war?

PSALM 116:15 | *The LORD cares deeply when his loved ones die.*

God created every person and God loves every person. Therefore anything that takes human life grieves God. So even if we conclude that there are times when war is permissible or necessary, remember that war should always be our last resort. And it is wise to be careful about glorifying war and reveling in death—even the death of our enemies.

How can I have peace of heart in a time of war?

PROVERBS 21:31 | *The horse is prepared for the day of battle, but the victory belongs to the LORD.*

It is the responsibility of those in the armed forces to be prepared. But ultimately the results of military maneuvers rest in God's hands.

PSALM 46:1-2 | *God is our refuge and strength, always ready to help in times of trouble. So we will not fear when earthquakes come and the mountains crumble into the sea.*

God is our ultimate protection, no matter what our circumstances are.

Will God ever do anything about war?

MICAH 4:3 | *The LORD will mediate between peoples and will settle disputes between strong nations far away. They will hammer their swords into plowshares and their spears into pruning hooks. Nation will no longer fight against nation, nor train for war anymore.*

PSALM 46:8-9 | *Come, see the glorious works of the LORD: . . . He causes wars to end throughout the earth. He breaks the bow and snaps the spear; he burns the shields with fire.*

When Jesus returns, war will be abolished forever. This is a cause for comfort and joy.

Promise from God MATTHEW 5:9 | *God blesses those who work for peace, for they will be called the children of God.*

WISDOM

See also **ADVICE/ADVISERS**

How will having wisdom help me?

ROMANS 12:2 | *Don't copy the behavior and customs of this world, but let God transform you into a new person by changing the way you think. Then you will learn to know God's will for you, which is good and pleasing and perfect.*

2 CORINTHIANS 10:4-5 | *We use God's mighty weapons, not worldly weapons, to knock down the strongholds of human reasoning and to destroy false arguments. We destroy every proud obstacle that keeps people from knowing God. We capture their rebellious thoughts and teach them to obey Christ.*

Wisdom transforms head knowledge into action based on common sense. Wisdom from God helps you develop a biblical outlook that penetrates the deceptive and distorted thoughts of the world.

PSALM 111:10 | *Fear of the LORD is the foundation of true wisdom. All who obey his commandments will grow in wisdom.*

PROVERBS 9:10 | *Knowledge of the Holy One results in good judgment.*

Wisdom is not simply knowing facts and figures; it is also understanding the filter through which those facts and figures should be used. Wisdom recognizes that an all-powerful, all-knowing God has designed a moral universe with consequences for good or sinful choices.

Wisdom begins with understanding your accountability to and your full dependence on your Creator. It's not *what* you know, but *who* you know.

How do I obtain wisdom?

JOB 28:12, 21 | *Do people know where to find wisdom? Where can they find understanding? . . . It is hidden from the eyes of all humanity.*

PROVERBS 9:10 | *Fear of the LORD is the foundation of wisdom. Knowledge of the Holy One results in good judgment.*

Wisdom is elusive unless you actively pursue it. When you know God, you know where to find it.

PSALM 5:8 | *Lead me in the right path, O LORD. . . . Make your way plain for me to follow.*

JAMES 1:5 | *If you need wisdom, ask our generous God, and he will give it to you. He will not rebuke you for asking.*

God promises to give wisdom to anyone who asks. You need not be embarrassed to ask God for the wisdom and direction you need.

PSALM 25:8-9 | *The LORD . . . leads the humble in doing right, teaching them his way.*

Wisdom comes more easily when you are humble.

PROVERBS 20:18 | *Plans succeed through good counsel.*

Wisdom often comes to you through the counsel of thoughtful, godly people.

Promise from God PROVERBS 1:23 | *Come and listen to my counsel. I'll share my heart with you and make you wise.*

WORDS

See also **COMMUNICATION**

Do my words really matter?

PSALM 15:1-3 | *Who may worship in your sanctuary, LORD? Who may enter your presence on your holy hill? Those who lead blameless lives and do what is right, speaking the truth from sincere hearts. Those who refuse to gossip or harm their neighbors or speak evil of their friends.*

JAMES 1:26 | *If you claim to be religious but don't control your tongue, you are fooling yourself, and your religion is worthless.*

Your words matter. What you say shows what kind of person you really are.

PROVERBS 11:11 | *Upright citizens are good for a city and make it prosper, but the talk of the wicked tears it apart.*

Your words affect the community at large, either greatly helping or hindering your group by what you say or don't say.

DEUTERONOMY 23:23 | *Once you have voluntarily made a vow, be careful to fulfill your promise to the LORD your God.*

JOSHUA 9:19-20 | *The leaders replied, "Since we have sworn an oath in the presence of the LORD, the God of Israel, we cannot touch them. This is what we must do. We must let them live, for divine anger would come upon us if we broke our oath."*

When you say you will do something, it is a binding commitment. Don't be careless about the "verbal contracts" you make.

PROVERBS 15:1 | *A gentle answer deflects anger, but harsh words make tempers flare.*

Words of blessing and wicked words are all very powerful.

How can I make the most impact with my words?

GENESIS 50:21 | *[Joseph] reassured them by speaking kindly to them.*

Speak kind words to others.

JOB 16:5 | *If it were me, I would encourage you. I would try to take away your grief.*

EPHESIANS 4:29 | *Let everything you say be good and helpful, so that your words will be an encouragement to those who hear them.*

Use words that build others up.

PROVERBS 15:4 | *Gentle words are a tree of life.*

PROVERBS 25:15 | *Patience can persuade a prince, and soft speech can break bones.*

Speak to others with gentleness.

PROVERBS 25:11 | *Timely advice is lovely, like golden apples in a silver basket.*

When the time is right, giving good advice can be very beneficial.

ECCLESIASTES 12:11 | *The words of the wise are like cattle prods— painful but helpful. Their collected sayings are like a nail-studded stick with which a shepherd drives the sheep.*

Use words to instruct and inspire others to be wise.

1 PETER 3:9 | *Don't repay evil for evil. Don't retaliate with insults when people insult you. Instead, pay them back with a blessing. That is what God has called you to do, and he will bless you for it.*

Use your words to bless even those who injure you.

ZECHARIAH 8:16 | *This is what you must do: Tell the truth to each other. Render verdicts in your courts that are just and that lead to peace.*

Speak truthfully.

What kinds of words should I avoid speaking?

EXODUS 22:28 | *You must not dishonor God or curse any of your rulers.*

Never curse God or anyone in leadership (or in any other situation, for that matter).

ECCLESIASTES 10:20 | *Never make light of the king, even in your thoughts. And don't make fun of the powerful, even in your own bedroom. For a little bird might deliver your message and tell them what you said.*

Do not mock or belittle those in leadership.

PSALM 34:12-13 | *Does anyone want to live a life that is long and prosperous? Then keep your tongue from speaking evil and your lips from telling lies!*

Avoid saying anything that is deceptive or false.

PROVERBS 18:8 | *Rumors are dainty morsels that sink deep into one's heart.*

Avoid spreading gossip or slander about other people.

PROVERBS 29:11 | *Fools vent their anger, but the wise quietly hold it back.*

Avoid speaking in the heat of anger; you will usually regret it later.

JAMES 4:11 | *Don't speak evil against each other, dear brothers and sisters. If you criticize and judge each other, then you are criticizing and judging God's law.*

Avoid criticizing other people.

Promise from God PROVERBS 20:15 | *Wise words are more valuable than much gold and many rubies.*

WORK

How should I view work?

GENESIS 1:27-28 | *God created human beings in his own image. . . . Then God blessed them and said, "Be fruitful and multiply. Fill the earth and govern it. Reign over the fish in the sea, the birds in the sky, and all the animals that scurry along the ground."*

Know that there is value and honor in work. God created people and gave them dominion over his creation. In other words, God created you for work. Work has always been meant to honor the Lord, to give people the dignity of having something important to do, and to bring blessings to others.

1 THESSALONIANS 4:11-12 | *Make it your goal to live a quiet life, minding your own business and working with your hands, just as we instructed you before. Then people who are not Christians will respect the way you live, and you will not need to depend on others.*

Your attitude toward work should include the goal of honoring God by the way you work, as well as supporting yourself and others.

PROVERBS 13:11 | *Wealth from get-rich-quick schemes quickly disappears; wealth from hard work grows over time.*

Honest, hard work is much better than schemes to get rich quickly.

Can I work too hard?

PSALM 39:6 | *All our busy rushing ends in nothing.*

ECCLESIASTES 5:3 | *Too much activity gives you restless dreams.*

While you are called to work hard, make sure that your work doesn't so preoccupy you that you endanger your health, your relationships, or your time with God.

ACTS 16:16 | *She was a fortune-teller who earned a lot of money for her masters.*

Don't allow your work to compromise your values.

EXODUS 16:23 | *This is what the LORD commanded: Tomorrow will be a day of complete rest, a holy Sabbath day set apart for the LORD.*

MARK 6:31 | *Jesus said, "Let's go off by ourselves to a quiet place and rest awhile."*

There is a time to stop your work in order to rest, to celebrate life, and to worship God.

Promise from God PHILIPPIANS 1:6 | *God, who began the good work within you, will continue his work until it is finally finished on the day when Christ Jesus returns.*

WORRY

See also **ADVERSITY, PROBLEMS**

How can I worry less?

PSALM 55:4-5 | *My heart pounds in my chest. . . . Fear and trembling overwhelm me, and I can't stop shaking.*

Worry and fear are normal responses to threatening situations, but often we imagine far worse scenarios than ever happen. Most worries never come true.

PSALM 62:6 | *[God] alone is my rock and my salvation, my fortress where I will not be shaken.*

Remembering that God's love and care for you are as solid as a rock can help keep your worries in perspective. He has everything under control.

MATTHEW 6:27 | *Can all your worries add a single moment to your life?*

Instead of adding more time or a better quality of life, worry diminishes your health and kills your joy.

PHILIPPIANS 4:6 | *Don't worry about anything; instead, pray about everything.*

1 PETER 5:7 | *Give all your worries and cares to God, for he cares about you.*

Talk to God openly about your worries. Hand them off to him as if to a consultant you totally trust or someone you have the utmost confidence in.

PHILIPPIANS 4:8-9 | *Fix your thoughts on what is true, and honorable, and right, and pure, and lovely, and admirable. Think about things that are excellent and worthy of praise. . . . Then the God of peace will be with you.*

COLOSSIANS 3:2 | *Think about the things of heaven, not the things of earth.*

Fix your thoughts on the power of God, not the problems of life. Worry will always change you for the worse; God has the power to change you and your circumstances for the better. Turn your attention away from negative, unbelieving thoughts to the positive, constructive thoughts of faith and hope.

EXODUS 14:13 | *Don't be afraid. Just stand still and watch the LORD rescue you today.*

Combat worry and anxiety by remembering and trusting what God, in his Word, has already promised to do for you.

JOHN 14:1-3 | *Don't let your hearts be troubled. Trust in God, and trust also in me. There is more than enough room in my Father's home. If this were not so, would I have told you that I am going to prepare a place for you? When everything is ready, I will come and get you, so that you will always be with me where I am.*

If you had ten million dollars in the bank, you wouldn't worry about providing for your family if you lost your job. In the same way, God has provided for your future by preparing a perfect place for you in heaven. Let that assurance keep you from panicking in today's storms. The outcome is certain.

Promise from God 1 PETER 5:7 | *Give all your worries and cares to God, for he cares about you.*

WORTH

See also **SELF-ESTEEM**

Am I really important to God?

GENESIS 1:26-27 | *God said, "Let us make human beings in our image, to be like us. They will reign over the fish in the sea, the birds in the sky, the livestock, all the wild animals on the earth, and the small animals that scurry along the ground." So God created human beings in his own image.*

PSALM 8:3-6 | *When I look at the night sky and see the work of your fingers . . . what are mere mortals that you should think about them . . . ? Yet you made them only a little lower than God and crowned them with glory and honor. You gave them charge of everything you made, putting all things under their authority.*

God made you in his own image—you are his treasure and masterpiece! You are invaluable to him.

PSALM 139:13 | *You made all the delicate, inner parts of my body and knit me together in my mother's womb.*

JEREMIAH 1:5 | *[The Lord said,] "I knew you before I formed you in your mother's womb. Before you were born I set you apart and appointed you as my prophet to the nations."*

God made you with great skill and crafted you with loving care. He showed how much value he places on you by the way he made you.

PSALM 139:17 | *How precious are your thoughts about me, O God. They cannot be numbered!*

Almighty God thinks wonderful thoughts about you all the time. He looks inside you and sees your real value.

PSALM 139:1-3 | *O LORD, you have examined my heart and know everything about me. You know when I sit down or stand up. You know my thoughts even when I'm far away. You see me when I travel and when I rest at home. You know everything I do.*

God values you so much that he watches over you no matter where you are or what you are doing. This tells you how special he thinks you are.

GALATIANS 3:26 | *You are all children of God through faith in Christ Jesus.*

GALATIANS 4:7 | *You are . . . God's own child. And since you are his child, God has made you his heir.*

God values you so much that he thinks of you as his child.

MATTHEW 28:20 | *[Jesus said,] "Be sure of this: I am with you always, even to the end of the age."*

God's Son promises to be with you always. Why would he want to be with you if he didn't value you?

Promise from God EPHESIANS 2:10 | *We are God's masterpiece. He has created us anew in Christ Jesus, so we can do the good things he planned for us long ago.*

EPILOGUE

I hope you have found—and will continue to find—wisdom and hope in this biblical guide. God's Word contains excellent directives on how to live life wherever you are, dealing with whatever circumstances you are facing, as I discovered during my thirty years of active duty in the US Air Force.

I was once asked in a mentoring session with a future four-star general what I wanted to achieve in my career. After careful thought and prayer, I decided that my three most important ambitions were (1) to serve with integrity; (2) to keep my family by my side; and (3) to finish well, having confidence that I had given it my all. I believe I met those goals, but how I wish I had had a copy of *TouchPoints for Those Who Serve* to help me along my path. Its succinct counsel would have been beneficial as I looked for the right words to share with those struggling to get back on track.

The powerful truth and words of encouragement found in Scripture provide a phenomenal tool for anyone who serves, whether as spouse, leader, commander, or chaplain. My prayer is that you will come back to this book again and again, finding wisdom for the issues you face.

Brigadier General David B. Warner, USAF (Ret)
Executive Director, Officers' Christian Fellowship

What is prayer? Prayer is talking to God about anything and everything. It's a privilege God wants you to utilize often, whether you feel close to him or not. Because God knows you so well—your joy as well as your troubles—nothing you say will surprise him. He just wants to hear what's on your heart. "Give all your worries and cares to God, for he cares about you" (1 Peter 5:7).

A SERVICE MEMBER'S PRAYER

Lord, I ask for courage . . .
  Courage to face and conquer my own fears.
  Courage to take me where others will not go.
I ask for strength . . .
  Strength of body to protect others.
  Strength of spirit to lead others.
I ask for dedication . . .
  Dedication to my job, to do it well.
  Dedication to my country, to keep it safe.
Give me, Lord, concern . . .
  For those who trust me and compassion for those
    who need me.
And, please, Lord . . .
  Through it all, be at my side.

AUTHOR UNKNOWN

THE STAR-SPANGLED BANNER

During the War of 1812 between the United States
and the British, American attorney Francis Scott Key
(1779–1843) was detained on an enemy troopship during
a twenty-five-hour bombardment of Fort McHenry on the
outskirts of Baltimore, Maryland. When dawn broke on
September 14, 1814, Key saw the American flag still flying
over the fort, inspiring him to write the lyrics to what
would become the US national anthem in 1931. Here are
the first and last stanzas.

> *O say can you see, by the dawn's early light,*
> *What so proudly we hail'd at the twilight's last gleaming,*
> *Whose broad stripes and bright stars through the*
>   *perilous fight*
> *O'er the ramparts we watch'd were so gallantly streaming?*
> *And the rocket's red glare, the bombs bursting in air,*
> *Gave proof through the night that our flag was still there,*
> *O say does that star-spangled banner yet wave*
> *O'er the land of the free and the home of the brave?*
>
> *O thus be it ever when freemen shall stand*
> *Between their lov'd home and the war's desolation!*
> *Blest with vict'ry and peace may the heav'n rescued land*
> *Praise the power that hath made and preserv'd us a nation!*
> *Then conquer we must, when our cause it is just,*
> *And this be our motto— "In God is our trust,"*
> *And the star-spangled banner in triumph shall wave*
> *O'er the land of the free and the home of the brave.*